Thy Maker Is Thy Husband

By

Gwendolyn Jackson

Copyright © 2001 by Gwendolyn Jackson
All rights reserved.
No part of this book may be reproduced, stored in a retrieval system, or transmitted by any means, electronic, mechanical, photocopying, recording, or otherwise, without written permission from the author.

Unless noted otherwise, all Scriptures quoted were taken from the Holy Bible, King James Version.

ISBN: 0-75961-528-4

This book is printed on acid free paper.

1stBooks - rev. 2/19/01

To my Father and Mother

Thank you both so much for being there for me through the storm and through the rain. I can never repay you for all you have done for me, but God has a crown waiting for you in Glory.

To my sons, Cornell & Charlie

Cornell, thank you for growing up and helping me during the hard times. God has something special in store for you. Charlie, you were the sunshine in my life during those rough times.

To my friend, Karen (Cookie) Richardson-Pleasant

Karen always said, "Girlfriend, you need to write a book!" Thanks Karen, for your inspiration. I finally wrote the book.

ABOUT THE BOOK

Denise Baker, a bright, intelligent, and spiritual young woman, had everything going for herself. Well on her way to becoming a successful young certified public accountant, Denise thought she had it all together until she was blind-sided by a fiery dart of the "wicked one". As you read this story, see how our human desires and emotions changed this young woman's life forever, from the time of her eighteenth birthday and for the next ten years. The desire to be married and have companionship took her to a place that only God could rescue her from. After reading this book, you will feel an urgency to share it with everyone you know. A life changing and thought provoking novel.

Behold I come quickly! Blessed is he who keeps the words of the prophecy of this book. –Revelation 22:7

THY MAKER IS THY HUSBAND

Rejecting Counsel 1

I Do 28

Marriage 101 38

Aboard A Sinking Ship 45

A House Divided 54

Single And Searching 74

Trick Or Treat 95

Stormy Weather 108

The Potter's House 129

Thy Maker Is Thy Husband 148

No Compromise 155

FOREWORD

It is not often that one reads a Christian based book that gives a perspective of God's purpose in such a candid and precise way. Minister Gwen Jackson, through her personal testimony has given every believer that has the nerves to pick up this book and read it, an opening to escape from the natural proclivities of the sinful flesh. She demonstrates how one can get off the course of God's purpose by looking for love in all the wrong places and how God's purpose will pursue you and ultimately convince you that no one can love you like Jesus. I believe everyone that reads this book, married or single, will be inspired to let God order their steps. It is written, "the steps of a good man are ordered by the Lord and he delights in His way" Psalms: 37:23

Bishop Calvin Scott, Pastor
Believers Temple Word Fellowship
Saint Louis, Missouri

CHAPTER 1

REJECTING COUNSEL

It was the spring of 1981. The alarm clock went off at 5:30 a.m. I didn't really want to get up that morning. The night before was my turn to close at the restaurant where I worked. Actually, at this point, it really didn't matter what I wanted to do. My parents had allowed me to work and go to school as long as my job didn't interfere with my education. I thought to myself as I jumped out of bed, if I don't get up for school, I may have to quit my job, then I won't be able to keep up with all of the latest fashions. That is all I did with my money–shop. I even sold candy at school for extra money. My father would tell me that I let money burn holes in my pockets. But I just couldn't seem to help it. I was a bonafide shop-aholic. I had all of the latest fashions in my two closets. It was a must that I owned all of the designer jeans that were in style. I didn't want to be found wearing an outfit that wasn't properly coordinated. I was pretty bad, but I loved every minute of it.

I was running late that morning. I had to run to catch the bus, the Lee/Riverroads. If I had missed my first bus, I would also have missed my connecting bus, the Kingshighway. There was no way I could be late again, or I'd get detention. I really enjoyed going to O'Fallon Technical High School. Being a junior had its advantages, such as the work study program I was in. As I walked down McRee, I heard the first bell ringing. I had to hurry so that I wouldn't be late for my first class. "Hey Kayla, I am running late, but I'll see you on second lunch. Meet me by the stairs." Kayla and I had been friends since our sophomore year. We had had lots of things in common last semester. We were in every class together except math. She and I talked a lot about the Lord. We even went to church together sometimes. Kayla was from a strict Pentecostal family. She wasn't allowed to wear pants; even when the temperature was below zero. I told her I would bring her some pants on the days it was really cold, but she said her parents wouldn't approve, even though the two of us agreed that God would not mind at all.

Kayla and I met for lunch as planned that day. Little did I know that this lunch hour would be like no other. As Kayla and I were coming out of the lunch line with our trays, someone called my name from the other end of the cafeteria. "Denise, Denise!" I couldn't see who was calling me. I always kept my glasses in my purse. Wearing glasses was **not** the cool thing to do. Kayla and I didn't see anyone, so we kept walking. We still heard this invisible person calling my name. I told Kayla to wait for me at the table while I went to see who it was. As I walked back to the other end of the cafeteria, I saw Brian Turner. "Hey Denise, baby!" he said.

"Hi Brian," I said.

"How have you been? Where have you been?"

All that was going through my mind was, 'He is so fine!' Brian said that he'd moved to Redwood City, California and was here visiting his family for Mother's Day.

"Denise, how have you been?" he said.

"Fine, going to school, church, working, shopping, the usual stuff." I said.

"Baby, I'm glad to hear you're doing well and I'll see you again before I leave, okay?"

"Okay." I said. With that, he walked away. I felt as if I'd seen Jesus Christ himself. Kayla said to me, "Who was that?"

"Brian Turner!" I said. She really didn't know him that well; he was only at O'Fallon during my freshman year. Brian and I had known each other since fourth grade. He was my first childhood boyfriend. When we were children, he used to tell me that when we grew up he was going to marry me and build me a glass house. Kayla and I laughed about how I looked when I got back from talking with Brian. I gave her play by play of our brief conversation.

Lunch hour was just about over and we had to go to the most boring class in the school, Ms. Mitchell's College Bound

Thy Maker Is Thy Husband

American History class. Kayla sat in front of me. So when Ms. Mitchell was not looking; I would scratch the dandruff from Kayla's scalp and then comb her hair. One day Ms. Mitchell caught me scratching Kayla's scalp and asked me what I thought I was doing. I told her, "Scratching dandruff."

She said, "That is disgusting and this is not a cosmetology class!" We thought we had better stop at that point. Ms. Mitchell did not play.

At 1:30 each day, I was able to leave school early to go to work. I thought it was pretty special being able to leave school before everyone else. As I walked up the street to catch my bus, I saw Brian again. He yelled from a distance. "Is your phone number 983-1838?"

"Yes," I yelled back. I couldn't believe he still remembered my phone number. He promised to call me later that night. I thought to myself, "Thank you, thank you, thank you!" I had already made up my mind, I wanted him and I was going to get him. I always got whatever I wanted when I put my mind to it. There was no doubt that I had the charm and the sex appeal to captivate him.

For a brief moment, I thought about how different my life was from this time last year. Back then, I wasn't dating, and was very involved in church. The passion of my life was witnessing to others about Christ and singing in our mass/radio choir. My life was completely dedicated to the work of the Lord, but it seemed like things began to change when I started dating. Though I loved God and enjoyed going to church, people would tell me that I acted too old fashioned and serious to be so young. They advised me to be more fun loving and enjoy being young. After hearing that so much, I started to wonder if maybe I was missing out on my youth and taking my spiritual life too seriously for someone my age. I thought I needed to experience things that I hadn't been able to do in the past. Being saved was all right, but I could get back into the things of God as I matured. Right then, I believed God wanted me to enjoy myself and to explore the lighter side of life.

Gwendolyn Jackson

My boyfriend Chris went to church and sang in the choir, but he wasn't as serious about God as I was. We met when we were sixteen and we both had a lot of peer pressure to deal with. We knew and understood what the word of God said about sex before marriage and how we should flee from youthful lust, but we couldn't resist the urge to try it. That's all it took, trying it just once. It was like a drug. That one time opened a door to many Just as he had planned, Brian called me at 9:00 p.m. sharp. I was on the phone talking to Chris. I clicked over and told Chris that it was my old friend from grade school, Brian, who was here visiting from California. I told Chris to call me back in half an hour. When I clicked back over, Brian began to tell me how good it was to see me and how he'd like to come by for a visit if it were possible. "BEEP," it was Chris calling me back again. This was his second time and his patience had grown short. He was very upset because Brian and I had been on the phone for over an hour. Because I was in seventh heaven, I told Chris to call me the next day. He was so fired up that he hung up on me. I didn't care. Brian and I talked until 2:00 a.m. I was as high as a kite from our conversation. I only slept for three hours before it was time for me to go to school. It didn't matter. I was seeing my dream come true right before my eyes. I couldn't wait to see Kayla at school that day to tell her everything. She was excited to hear what had happened and we laughed and joked about it. Yet, at the same time she saw that I was drifting further and further away from God and that made her hurt for me.

Meanwhile, Chris called and cursed me out. He went completely off on me. He said that if Brian showed up at my house he would kick our butts. I wasn't trippin off anything he was saying. I didn't know what was wrong with him–we weren't married. I could have friends if I wanted to. If he couldn't understand that, he was just out of luck.

Brian showed up at my house on time that day. I was in my room putting on a new outfit I bought at Paul Harris. I thought I looked pretty cute and I hoped he would think the same. My

Thy Maker Is Thy Husband

mother and older sister Joyce let Brian in. They were almost as excited as I was. Brian was so charming, polite and handsome. "Good evening Mrs. Baker, Joyce. How are you all doing?" he said as he embraced them both. Neither one of them had seen Brian since grade school. My mother and sister were both asking him a thousand questions a minute. They asked about California and told him how handsome he'd become. I was standing back wishing they would cut it short and let me entertain my company downstairs, alone! Finally, Brian and I were able to go to the basement. Before we could get to the bottom of the stairs, he embraced me with a warm and passionate kiss. I thought I was seeing fireworks like on the 4th of July. At that point, Chris was history. After a wonderful two hours with Brian, he had to leave. He promised me that he would be back to see me again before he left. I couldn't believe it was happening. I felt as if it was the greatest day of my life and the beginning of a beautiful new romance.

The next evening, I had choir rehearsal. I hadn't been singing much lately. To be honest, I really felt funny singing because I wasn't so sure if that was what God wanted me to do. I couldn't sing that well and I definitely wouldn't be cutting a record any time soon. I would make tonight my last rehearsal and check back with the Lord for some new direction. Brian called me when I was getting ready for bed. I told him that maybe I would have a sudden case of the stomach flu Monday morning. That way, I could see him at 9:00 a.m. after everyone had gone. We both said we couldn't wait to see each other. As planned, I got out of bed pretending to get ready for school. Then I said to my mom, "Mama that meatloaf you cooked last night didn't agree with my system. I had diarrhea all last night. I think I had better stay home." I was lying of course.

Mama said, "Go on and stay home Denise. Hmm. It sure is funny no one else got an upset stomach. Your system is funny."(Oh man, it worked!). I just hoped God wouldn't make me sick for real. I hated to lie, but I knew lying was the only way I was going to be able to see Brian.

Gwendolyn Jackson

The doorbell rang and my heart started beating fast. I was a little nervous, because I knew something very special was about to happen. "Good morning Brian," I said.

"Good morning Denise, my love," he said. I had prepared a wonderful breakfast for us because I wanted to start the day off right. Brian kept telling me how good my cooking was and how he hoped I would be able to cook like that when we were married. My stomach got a knot in it. I said to myself, "I can't believe he is thinking that far ahead." As we washed the dishes, Brian began to caress my neck and shoulders. When I responded, we started slowly up the stairs to my bedroom. That day, Brian and I made love for the first time. It seemed so perfect, so right. In my mind, I could not see anything wrong with such beautiful affection shared between childhood sweethearts. The only thing it could be was perfect. At that moment, all of the lessons that I'd learned in Sunday school, all the sermons that Bishop Jenkins had preached and all that my parents had taught me about sex before marriage, no longer applied to this new found love between Brian and me. Yet, I hoped and prayed that I wouldn't step one notch backward from God.

It was getting close to noon and I wasn't sure what time my sister Joyce would be home. That would be all I needed, her catching us alone. She was always calling me **Miss Goody Two Shoes** anyway. If she found out, she'd have a field day with it. I told Brian that he should leave before she popped up.

Three weeks later, it was Memorial Day and my seventeenth birthday. Brian was coming with my family and me on a picnic. I went to the mall and got T-shirts made that said "Brian and Denise, Together for Always." We were going to wear our jeans and shirts to the picnic. I got up early that morning ready to show off my fine new man. I don't know why, but I kept getting the strangest feeling that he wasn't going to show. I almost didn't get the shirts made, but because I wanted it to work out so badly, I got them anyway. Sure enough, my female intuition was right. Ring, Ring, "Hey sweetheart." It was Brian.

Thy Maker Is Thy Husband

"Hi," I said, waiting for the other shoe to drop. I could tell by the tone of his voice that he was about to break our date.

"Listen, my mother wants me to go to Jefferson Barracks cemetery with her to visit my grandmother's grave. I'm sorry babe, but I won't be able to go with you."

I was so upset with him, that I said, "Brian, just forget it! As a matter of fact, don't even bother calling me anymore. You're probably faking," I said to him. "It is mighty funny that you haven't been back since you got what you wanted from me. I guess you have to finish your rounds, goodbye dog!" and I hung up. I had the worse birthday that I could remember. I felt like a fool going around telling all of my friends how Brian and I were going to spend my birthday together. They had all told me, "Girl I heard he was a "dog" anyway! All he wants to do is get in your panties and then he's out of there." I thought they were just being jealous, but maybe they were right.

It had been a while since I had asked the Lord to help me with my schoolwork. I wasn't too sure that he would, since I hadn't been practicing my faith lately. Final exam day was upon me and I was dreading Ms. Mitchell's final exam. I hadn't paid much attention this last semester, because of my involvement with both Chris and Brian. Maybe by some miracle, I would pass the class. When Ms. Mitchell passed out the exam, I looked at it and didn't have a clue.

At that point, I knew that I was going to fail the class. Not to my surprise, I did. An "F." A big fat "F." I couldn't believe it! I had never made an "F" in my entire life. My father was going to have a fit! I decided to keep it a secret as long as I could. I was really bumming now. First, I blew off my friend Chris, I let Brian play me for a fool and now I failed my American History class. I wondered if things could get any worse.

As I rode the bus home from work a week later, I thought about Brian. I knew that he was going back to California. I thought to myself, it would have been nice if Brian and I were still together like in a fairytale. That's just what it was – a fairytale. My sister Joyce met me at the bus stop since it was almost dark by the time I got home. We chitchatted about the days' happenings. She told me that she and a customer at Kentucky Fried Chicken (her job) almost got into a fight, because this white lady called her a nigger. I was surprised Joyce hadn't followed the customer home. Joyce would do anything, especially when it came to prejudiced people. When I walked in the door, my mama called me to her room. My heart began to race.

"He called from Colorado somewhere and said to tell you he will call you in a few days." After hearing that news, I started wondering if things would work out for Brian and me after all.

But as the weeks passed, I didn't hear from him. I started going out with Darnell. We worked and attended O'Fallon Tech together. He was a lot of fun to be with, but he was a little too silly for me. He was okay to be with for the moment, but I couldn't see anything happening on the serious tip. Darnell could play the guitar. Sometimes he would make up songs for me. I liked Darnell as my special friend, but that was it.

After breaking up with Chris and being dissed by Brian, I returned to my church family. I read my bible more and began my prayer life again. I was feeling clean on the inside.

That summer, my family and I took a long trip to Georgia. It was about as hot as they say Hell is going to be. I didn't even want to leave the hotel, so I had plenty of time to think about getting myself together and making plans for the coming year. At seventeen, I realized that the things I'd been involved with lately, especially the sexual relations, had opened a door that I wasn't sure could be easily shut. But I knew I could get it together. Why, just recently, Darnell and I had a lot of opportunities to "get busy" and we didn't. I wanted to, in a way, but at the same time, I wanted us to stay good friends. I didn't want our "getting intimate" to change that. Maybe I was getting things back under control.

After a long, hot and boring trip to Georgia, we finally were heading back to the Show-me-State. On the way back, we stopped in Memphis to see the kinfolks and that was pretty cool.

Thy Maker Is Thy Husband

They were always trying to feed you that southern style cooking: turnip greens and hot water cornbread. I didn't eat that kind of stuff, but I did eat the fried chicken!

September was only two weeks away. Senior year had finally arrived. I even scored high enough on my SAT to be accepted into Washington University, an Ivy League university in St. Louis, Missouri. My only obstacle was taking that American History class over again. I couldn't graduate until I passed it. I had planned to major in Accounting with a minor in Business Administration. My application was on its way. Mr. Perkins, my boss had made me shift manager at his restaurant and I figured that I could continue working there once I started college to help my parents with expenses.

The school year had begun and things were going well. I was still in the Work-Study Program, so I was dismissed from school each day at 10:30 a.m. One day, my guidance counselor called me into her office and asked me if I would be interested in working at City Hall in downtown St. Louis. I told her I would give it a try. And, try it I did, but it was not my cup of tea. After a couple of weeks, I went back to see if I could use my job at the restaurant as my work-study credit. I was allowed to do so. I knew that would be an easy "A." Mr. Perkins really liked me. He always told me that I was a very hard worker and that I had a good head on my shoulders. He said if I stayed on the path I was on, I would be the owner of a business someday.

Fall was my favorite time of the year. I loved seeing the trees with all of their different colors. I especially loved going to the park and crunching the leaves under my feet. I spent quite a bit of time alone those days. Since that encounter with Brian, I'd sort of lost interest in socializing. My Friday nights consisted of watching Dallas and Falcon Crest; my two favorite shows. One night, while watching TV, a Rice-a-Roni commercial came on. It showed the cable cars in San Francisco and it made me think of Brian for about the tenth time that day. I said to myself, "I wonder if he has been thinking of me?" We hadn't spoken in almost four months. It wasn't twenty minutes after I saw the

Gwendolyn Jackson

cable car on the commercial the telephone rang. It was Brian. I couldn't believe it! It was almost as though our hearts were speaking and calling out to each other. The first thing he said to me: "Denise, baby, I have missed you so much. I only waited to call because I wasn't sure if you would even talk to me again. I knew I hurt you by not going with you on Memorial Day and you felt I'd just used you. I know for a fact that I love you and I want you to be mine." After hearing all of that, I wasn't sure what to think. I knew I badly wanted to be with him. So I thought it was worth giving our relationship another try. I told Brian that I missed him too. I was so glad that he called me and I hoped we could start all over. Brian said he wanted me in his life for always. He asked me if I would consider changing my plans for college and apply at San Francisco State University. He wanted me to be as close to him as possible. I told him I would call on Monday to get information regarding the school. At last, my charming prince was in my life once again. This time, maybe forever. By the time Brian and I finished talking, he had said so many things, that he had my head spinning. I had to let everything soak in. I thought I would wait until the next day to tell my mother and father that I was considering going to San Francisco State University. I already knew they wouldn't be too thrilled about me going so far away, though I knew I could take care of myself very well.

Over breakfast the next morning, I asked myself how to bring up the subject. The first thing my daddy would say: "Girl don't you be trying to go all the way to California to go to school. That nappy-headed boy ain't going anywhere!" My mama would say: "Now Denise, you know how they have all them earthquakes in California. I don't know about you going to school out there. You'll have to see what your daddy says." I thought I might as well find out now. "Mama, Daddy, I have been thinking about contacting San Francisco State University to get some information regarding their degree programs. I'm quite sure they offer the same things that Wash U. does and by the

Thy Maker Is Thy Husband

way, Brian said I could save on the housing and stay with him in Redwood City and ..."

Before I could finish, my daddy said, "I am not going to have you living with no nappy headed boy in California. You just keep your butt right here and go to school."

"But daddy, I want to be near Brian."

"Denise, I don't want to hear nothing else about California."

"Okay, fine!" I was pretty hot. I pushed back from the table, slammed my plate in the sink and stomped upstairs to my room and slammed the door. I waited for a minute to see if I had gotten away with what I'd just done. I didn't hear any footsteps, so I must have gotten that one off. All I could think about was not being able to be near Brian. I wanted to call him so badly, but we could only talk twice a week. I began to write Brian a letter to tell him that my parents were not going for the idea of me going to college in California and when they heard about the idea of my living with him, that canceled Christmas!

My parents were strict Baptist folks from the South and I knew they were not going to agree with the arrangements that Brian and I had made. I was so angry with them. I did not know what to do, so I called my friend Donna. She and I had been friends since the sixth grade. I was crying when I called her. "What's wrong Dee?" I told her that my daddy wouldn't let me go to college in California. Donna said, "You should have known "T" wasn't going for that!" Donna had nicknames for my whole family. She said my mother (whom she calls Nunie), wouldn't sleep at night with her baby in California. Donna said that maybe God had a reason for me not going. I had no idea why God wouldn't want me to be with the person I loved more than anyone. I felt this was so right, even though during the time Brian and I weren't talking, I had been reading scriptures about not being unequally yoked with unbelievers in God. Just because he didn't go to church all of the time, didn't make him a non-believer. He went to a Lutheran church when he did attend.

It was Tuesday evening now. Three days had passed since I'd gotten the bomb dropped on me. While I was waiting for

Brian to call, all I kept thinking about was, I wonder if he will come back to St. Louis to be with me. I knew there was no way that he would want to come back to this dull town. The only place to take visitors when they came was to the Gateway Arch, the mall, or to Six Flags. It was not as exciting as it is in California. The phone rang. Depressed, I said, "Hey Babe."

Brian immediately said, "Oh no, what's wrong with my baby?" I told him that the ole dude wasn't going for it. As far as my coming to California to go to school; we might as well forget that for now. There was a long pause, then Brian said to me "Denise, I love you so much. I have loved you since fifth grade and I want to be with you always. I know now that the only way it can happen is if ..."

I said to Brian, " If what?"

"Denise Baker, will you be my wife – will you marry me?" I couldn't believe what I was hearing. Brian repeated himself, "Denise, will you marry me?" I was so shocked, amazed and overwhelmed, that I said yes to him about twenty times. We both were smiling on the phone, crying tears of joy, that a childhood dream was going to come true. Then suddenly, I snapped back into reality. I knew that there was no way my parents were going to give their blessing to me getting married at eighteen and risking my college education. The fact of the matter was that they didn't even know a lot about Brian and his family, so that would make them skeptical. Even though Brian had asked me to marry him and I had accepted, we still had a lot of hoops to jump through.

Thanksgiving holiday was approaching and I thought about asking my parents about going to California. I said to myself that I wouldn't plan a certain day to ask them. Whenever I feel it is right, that's when I'll ask. It was the last day of school before the holiday. Crystal, my friend, came home with me from school and we talked a mile a minute on the bus about my upcoming wedding. My friends at school couldn't believe that I had the nerve to go through with it. As Crystal and I walked down the street, I could see my brother's car in the driveway. I said to

Thy Maker Is Thy Husband

myself, today is the day that I ask for my parents' permission and blessings. For a minute, I wondered isn't it usually the groom's job to ask the father of the bride to take his daughter's hand in marriage and for their blessing? Hopefully, Brian had just let this part slip his mind and I figured that it really didn't matter. This is the eighties. Women are taking the lead now! When Crystal and I got to my house, I asked Crystal to go up to my room and wait for me. My mama was sitting on the toilet and I went to the door and came right out with it. "Mama, Brian asked me to marry him last night and I said yes. Is it okay with you?" My mama was glad that she was already on the toilet, or she might have had some problems.

"Denise, have you lost your mind? I know you must be joking. Why in the world would you want to get married at eighteen? You are still a child. You have always been in such a hurry to grow up. Denise, I am telling you that you had better slow down before you bite off more than you can chew." I thought I would compare my situation to that of my parents' and see how that would go over. I reminded my mother that she and my father had married young. She was only nineteen. My mama said to me, "Denise, times were different then. We had a child and things were just different. We probably were too young ourselves." Boy, I tell you, all parents do is constantly compare what they did to the things that their children want to do in their lives. I wish they would stop comparing their situation to ours. Just because their dreams sometimes became nightmares, didn't necessarily mean that the same thing would happen to us.

I went to my room where Crystal was waiting for me. "As it stands, my mother is definitely against my getting married."

"But she said, as she always does, "Whatever your daddy says." My next task was to catch my daddy in a good mood, which was pretty rare. Between his job and working at our small family grocery store, things got pretty crazy at times. My father tried hard to keep the peace between himself and my uncle who owned the store. Two of my uncles were alcoholics and things got pretty heated at the store at times. I remember times when we had to close the store in the middle of the day because all of the arguing and fussing that went on. So my daddy didn't have too many occasions to be in a good mood. I believed I would catch him in one soon. Normally on payday he was pretty cool. I decided to ask him on Friday. Friday evening I was not scheduled to work, so I thought a good way to talk to daddy was to go over to the store to help put up stock. I thought that day was the pick of the week (if there was one). My daddy was at the counter finishing up with some customers. I thought that was the perfect moment. "Daddy, Brian called me the other day from California. He asked me to marry him." My daddy had a very unconcerned look on his face. "Did you hear what I said?"

"Yeah, I heard you. Don't the boy know that he is supposed to call and speak to me about marrying you?" I really wasn't sure why Brian hadn't called and talked with him. I just told him that Brian must have forgotten. My father asked when all of this was supposed to take place. I told him that we would like to do it after my graduation, probably sometime in June. Brian asked if it would be okay for me to come to San Francisco at Christmas to be officially engaged. My father's answer was, "Whatever your mama says." I couldn't believe that was his answer! It was never what my mama said. Daddy was always THE TOP DOG, THE HEAD HONCHO. He always had to have the last say. One of the most serious things that I had ever asked, or probably would ever ask his permission for and his response was "Whatever your mama says?" I am home free now! After all, I was her BABY GIRL. If that would make me happy, she would GO ALONG WITH IT. "It's on like a pot of neckbones." I couldn't wait to call Brian that night with the fantastic news. California here I come! The only thing now was that I would have to work like a Hebrew slave, day and night, to pay for my ticket at Christmas.

Brian worked at the neighborhood store in Redwood City, right across the street from his apartment. Brian had been promoted to Assistant Manager of the store. I never could figure out why Brian hadn't offered to help pay for my plane ticket. I

Thy Maker Is Thy Husband

said I wouldn't make a big deal out of it since he had bills to pay himself. So I really didn't mind the sacrifice of working overtime to pay for my plane ticket. It was worth all of that!

It was just two weeks before Christmas. I received my first credit card in the mail from Famous Barr. I was so excited, I almost did a backwards flip. I was in a hurry to go out and do some major shopping for Christmas. Before I could get out of the door, my mother said, "Denise, now don't you go out and charge that card up to the limit. Those credit cards can get you in a lot of trouble if you are not careful with them." I told my mama not to worry so much. I would pay for everything that I charged. She didn't have to worry about me. My mama just looked at me, shook her head and told me to be careful.

I thought I was in "Lifestyle of the Rich and Famous." I shopped until I dropped that day. I bought new jeans, a coat, perfume, new clothes for Brian and some pretty nice gifts for my other family members. By the time I finished shopping, I'd charged over one thousand dollars! I knew that was too much, but it sure felt good. I said that after I came back from California, I would work very hard to pay off the charge amount before Brian and I got married.

Christmas Eve, I was making last minute preparations for my trip. Brian's mother and stepfather, Mr. and Mrs. Williams were coming over. I would meet them for the first time. Brian's mother had some things for me to take to Brian, his brother and two sisters. I wanted to make a good first impression. My mother let Mr. and Mrs. Williams in to the house. I wanted them to greet one another before I came downstairs. I heard them laughing and talking, so I said it's about time, time to meet my future in-laws. I wondered if she would be the nightmare I had heard some mother-in-laws were. She really wouldn't have the chance to be my nightmare, because we would be on the West Coast. Mrs. Williams was nothing like I thought. She was a very attractive lady with light blonde hair. Thank God she had a light complexion, because if she had been one of those dark-skinned sisters with all of that blonde hair, it would have been over! Mr. Williams was just your regular kind of guy, who didn't mind having a cocktail or two. They both seemed pretty cool and down to earth. Of course, Mrs. Williams started out saying, "So you've gotten my son hooked and you're off to live in California."

I smiled and said, "I don't know about having him hooked, but I know that we want to be together forever and if that means moving away, a woman must do what a woman must do." Mr. Williams said, "Watch out now, the little lady knows what she's got to do!" We all sat around for a couple of hours getting acquainted. By the time the Williams left, it seemed so perfect, everything was going well, but I still felt a sense of guilt. I wasn't sure God was with me in this. I was still trying to convince myself that everything was okay between the Lord and me. Still, I was starting to feel that something was missing within me. I was having a hard time being completely and totally happy about all of this. "Enough of this," I thought. "I am getting married to the man of my dreams."

I could see the sun shining through my window. It was Christmas Day, 1981. I loved Christmas. I loved the family gatherings that the holiday season brought. I had to get up early for our third annual family Christmas breakfast. It's really a nice event for the family members and close friends. We always have the breakfast at our house. We sang Christmas carols. We had a family prayer, which Grandpa Ted always led. His prayers seemed an hour long. My mama says Grandpa Ted prayed long when they were kids back home. We had all kinds of good food, homemade biscuits made from scratch, stewed potatoes, slab bacon, grits and so many other delicious foods that I couldn't begin to name them. After breakfast, we would all gather in the living room and share testimonies about what God had done during the year. I didn't think it was time to say anything about my engagement. You know how family can be, they will pretend that they are happy for you, but then will say something else when you are not around. I knew this would hot be gossip, me getting married at eighteen. Oh well, I really didn't give a hill of beans what they thought. I just sat quietly and listened to the others testify and some "test-a-lie."

When I finished packing, it looked like I was taking everything with me, except the kitchen sink. When the phone rang, it was Brian. He was calling to wish me a Merry Christmas. He said it was the best Christmas he'd ever had. He said he'd received a gift that could not be bought with money, ME!! I was so touched by what he had said that it made me more excited and happy knowing I would be with him this time tomorrow. I told him how much I loved him and that we would celebrate Christmas everyday while I was visiting him. I said goodbye and that I'd see him the next day. I went to bed early because I wanted to look my very best for my honey the next day. I thought if I went to bed by eight o'clock, morning would come sooner. I knew this was going to be great.

I woke up every three hours during the night to make sure I hadn't overslept. I knew that I had to do something to get some sleep, or I would look like seven miles of bad highway tomorrow. I got up and took some cough medicine thinking to myself, "I'll be in dreamland in a few minutes."

As I turned over in bed, I could see the sun beaming through my window. After seven months, I was going to be with my baby. I was really on my way to California to become engaged. My life would no longer be the same. My mother and father were a little bit excited about me going on the trip. They helped me make sure that I had all of my belongings. I had four suitcases to check at the airport.

It was a beautiful winter morning. The snow hadn't completely melted and the sky was the prettiest blue that I had seen in a while. It was very, very, cold; only ten degrees!!! In a few short hours, it would be sixty. My father pulled up to the curb to check my bags with the skycap. I had to pay an extra charge because I had too many pieces of luggage. I didn't care. The skycap wasn't going to receive a tip. I just hoped they wouldn't be ignorant and lose my bags on purpose.

Gwendolyn Jackson

I couldn't believe this was happening. I thought to myself, I am really on the plane to see Brian. As I was saying these words to myself, the flight attendants were preparing for departure. One got on the microphone, welcoming us to TWA, flight 223, to San Francisco. I had been assigned to seat 8-C, next to a young, chubby, freckled- faced white lady from Michigan. I could tell she would make the ride go by quickly. She had black hair that was cut short, "go-go" boots and a short, white skirt and blouse. This young lady started talking the minute she sat down and didn't stop until we landed four hours later in San Francisco.

As we began to descend into the Bay area, I couldn't believe how beautiful it was. It looked like a place on the other side of the world. A feeling of euphoria came over me. All I could think was, "This is a dream come true." My stomach began to roll. I thought I had better do a last minute makeup check. My honey was down there waiting for me, just a few feet away. I walked slowly down the jet way, getting my last minute thoughts together.

Brian was waiting at the end of the jet way and all I could do was drop my bags and hug him as tight as I could. He looked fine as he had seven months ago and I thought he was pleased with his "Nicey Pooh"(his pet name for me). A couple of his buddies were waiting to take me for a quick spin. Brian said, "Baby, I'm so happy to see you, I hope this week will be the best one both of us have ever had and I am going to make sure you enjoy every minute of your visit in your soon to be home." Waiting in the car was BJ and Keith. Keith was Brian's best friend. I could tell that they had been looking out of the window checking me out. When I got in the car, Keith said to me, "So this is Denise, the lady I feel like I know already? Brian talks about you twenty-four/seven." I blushed all over knowing my baby talked about me to his friends.

As we were leaving the airport heading for the Oakland Bay Bridge, Brian's friend, BJ lit a marijuana joint. I turned around and said, "What are you doing?" That's the one thing that I didn't do, mess around with drugs. Then Brian said, "Denise,

Thy Maker Is Thy Husband

baby, it's okay. It's just a joint, everyone smokes a little weed every now and then." Then BJ passed the joint on to Brian and he took three long hits off it. I didn't want to say anything in front of his friends, but I was saying to myself, I can't wait until we drop them off. Nevertheless, I was enjoying the ride across the bridge to Oakland. I was so caught up in the beauty of my surroundings, that I wasn't really upset about Brian hitting the joint.

Finally, we were alone. I said to Brian, "Sweetheart, I didn't know you smoked weed."

"Don't you remember in seventh grade when my brother and I would steal joints from my old man and get high going to school?"

"Yeah, I remember," I said. "But I didn't think you still did that." Brian then told me not to worry that smoking a little weed and drinking brew every so often didn't make him a bad guy. Brian promised me that he wouldn't over do it. We then kissed and hugged. We thought we would wait until he got off work to make up for the last seven months, but we just couldn't wait. It was well worth the wait!!!

Brian and I dozed off to sleep. The next thing we knew, he had only fifteen minutes left to get to work. Luckily, he only had to go across the street. Brian and his sister, Carla shared an apartment. I hadn't had a chance to meet her yet. Brian told me to just make myself at home and his sister would be back in a couple of hours. He kissed me goodbye and was off to work until eleven that night. Eight long hours without him, but he told me to come across the street to the store if I started missing him.

When Brian left, I sat down in the chair and stared out the window, looking at the beautiful skyline, the palm trees and the bay right down the street. Everything was so nice, I felt a little sad, because I was so shocked seeing Brian smoking that joint. He told me that he didn't get high much and I wanted to believe him, but he hit that joint like a pro. "Maybe I had better start praying to be sure this is the road I should be on." I thought things would not have worked out this good if things weren't

Gwendolyn Jackson

meant to be. Maybe I was just worrying for nothing. At least I hoped so.

I fell asleep on the couch and Carla came through the door singing one of Luther Vandross' latest tunes, smoking a cigarette. She shook my shoulders and said, "Hey Denise." I woke up hoping I didn't have any sleep juice all over my face.

"Hi Carla," I hugged her and told her it was really nice to finally meet her face to face.

"So Denise, you and my baby brother are getting married. I know you're going to take good care of each other." Carla was telling me that Brian and I had started something. She was getting married in February to a guy that played for Rick James. She was moving up in the world. After Carla said that, I had a strange feeling come over me. I guess it was starting to sink in. I was getting married!!

I turned on the radio to see what kind of stations they had in the Bay area. I had recently started listening to secular music again. Up until last summer, I had only listened to gospel music. I never really understood what the big deal was all about. Listening to music is good for the mind. As I was changing the stations, I ran across a religious station. I heard the minister preaching about your house being built on a rock. He said in his message that if one's house was built on sand, it was sure to fall. I remembered that Scripture in Matthew 7:26-27. Maybe I would read it later. I have always believed that when you hear the word of God by accident, you should read it because it may have a message for you. "I hope they have a Bible here," I thought, since I hadn't brought one with me. I changed the station and found a real nice jazz station. They were jamming. I cooled out the rest of the evening listening to music.

The sun was beginning to set over the Pacific Ocean. I still felt like I was in paradise. I was counting the hours until it was time for Brian to get off work. I wanted to cook him a special dinner, but the fridge was pretty bare. I figured we could go around the corner to the Italian restaurant and have a nice quiet romantic dinner. Finally, eleven o'clock came and at exactly

Thy Maker Is Thy Husband

11:04p.m., Brian walked through the door. We didn't even say hello, he just held me in his arms and kissed me for five minutes. I tried to stop and tell him that I'd made plans for dinner, but eating was not on his mind and it really wasn't on mine either. We just wanted to make up for lost time and it was a night that I would never forget.

I couldn't believe how fast the week had gone by. It was New Year's Eve, 1981. I was starting to get just a little bit nervous. Brian hadn't proposed to me yet! My father would crucify me if I came back from this trip and Brian and I weren't engaged. I kept telling myself, "Don't worry, you'll be engaged before the year is over." Brian's older sister, Shirley was going to take us out for breakfast. I really hit it off with her. She and I were both motherly types. I was happy that she would be here when I came to live in California. After breakfast, Brian and I went on a long drive around the area. Brian decided that he would take me across the Golden Gate Bridge to Sausalito. It was so beautiful there. We found a nice, romantic spot overlooking the Pacific Ocean. We got out of the car and found a giant rock to sit on. Everything seemed so perfect. I was with the one person I loved more than anyone in the world and we were right in the midst of paradise. I was thinking so many things. I was hoping that somehow the Lord would understand the bond that Brian and I shared and bless our marriage. I hoped that when I returned and met with Bishop Jenkins, that he would give us his blessings too. As I drifted far off in thought, Brian knelt down before me and took my hand. My heart was beating two hundred times a minute. Brian looked up into my eyes as he held my hand said, "Denise, my love, my first love from childhood, the woman that I want to spend the rest of my life with, will you marry me? Will you be mine forever?"

I got down on my knees and said to him, "Brian, my love, my childhood sweetheart, I remember when we were in fifth grade, you told me that I was going to be your wife someday. Today, many years later, what you said is about to come true. Yes, Brian my love, I will marry you. I will be your wife." We embraced one another. Another beautiful sunset was beginning over the ocean and we started to head back to town.

Carla had planned a little celebration for that evening. I was quite sure this would be pretty "live." As I expected, the celebration Carla had planned was just like I had thought it would be. Brian and Carla celebrated big time. They popped champagne and made about fifteen toasts to everyone. I wasn't really a drinker, so I just sipped on a glass of champagne. As the partying continued, Brian pulled a shoebox lid from under the sofa, inside was some marijuana and some kind of brown stuff. I asked Brian what it was and he said that it was just a little hash that he mixed with marijuana. It would make the weed and the high would last a little longer. It was bad enough seeing him get high the other day and now he was mixing weed with that other mess. I told Brian, "I am not going for my man doing drugs." Brian kept assuring me that he only did it for fun every once in a while. He said that after being with him all week, that I should be able to see that too. He told me to trust and believe in him and he was not going to do anything to jeopardize our future together.

By eleven o'clock, Brian and Carla had gone through two bottles of champagne. Brian was stretched out on his waterbed. Dick Clark and I were counting down to the New Year. I jumped up and said, "No, I am going to bring 1982 in with my husband to be." I went to Brian's room and began to shake the bed. All of a sudden, he jumped up and ran to the bathroom and threw up all over the place. It was a mess. The pizza, the champagne, everything was all over the floor and toilet. I had to clean up the mess. I said to myself, "Are these things going to be a part of my duties as a future wife?" I felt like telling Brian to clean up his own mess, but I thought I would make a good first impression and show him that I loved him enough to clean up his vomit.

Brian and I stayed up all night. Loving on each other, talking and planning our wedding and our future. We both could not believe that this fairytale we'd talked about as children was

Thy Maker Is Thy Husband

actually coming true. The only sad part about our last night together was that we would not see each other again for five long months. We wondered how we would live without each other that long. Nevertheless, we had to do what we had to do.

My flight back home to St. Louis was scheduled to leave San Francisco at 10:30 a.m. Brian and I got up very early after getting only a couple of hours of sleep. Both of us were very quiet. Brian had to run an errand while I packed my things. I had brought so much stuff with me that I had to leave a piece of my luggage and some of my sweaters with Brian. At least he would have something everyday to remind him of me. I heard Richard, Brian's brother coming through the door. He hadn't been around much since I had been here. He came in and said, "What's up Sis?" I told him I was wondering the same thing since he hadn't come by and spent ten minutes with me while I'd been in town. Richard told me not to take it personally. He said to be frank about the whole thing, that he thought Brian was "full of it." Richard felt as though Brian just wanted to marry me because he thought my family had a lot of money and because Carla was moving to Dallas. Richard also said that Brian probably loved me in his own way, but he really didn't believe Brian was getting married in the name of love. I told Richard to go on with his negative mess. I asked him if he was sure he wasn't just envious of Brian because he would be the only one not married? He looked at me and said to give him a break. He told me he wished us well and he would see me in June. On the way to the airport, we stopped at this little place on the San Francisco Bay called Coyote Pointe. It was a secluded area on the beach. Carla and Shirley were going with us to the airport. The two of them walked in the other direction to give Brian and me some privacy. It was a very chilly and breezy morning. Brian said to me, "Denise, I know that this is a big step that both of us are about to take. We both are very young, but I know that the two of us can do anything we set our minds to. Denise baby, I promise you that I am going to take good care of you. I love you so much and I can't wait to see you again." Brian left me speechless, which was very rare. I told him that I loved him too and that as soon as I got back to St. Louis, I would call Bishop Jenkins to ask him to marry us. Then I would call Brian to let him know the date the Bishop had given me. I also told Brian about the conversation I had with Richard. Brian told me not to worry and that his brother was jealous of him. He also told me that Richard couldn't stand the thought of him having found a good woman or real happiness. Brian said he would get with Richard later that day.

It was time to say our final good-bye. Brian hugged me real tight and told me to take care and to save myself for him. I told him to do the same. I wasn't quite sure why he said that, but I didn't want anyone else but him. He didn't have to worry about that. Carla and Shirley hugged me and welcomed me into the family. I walked down the jet way backwards waving good-bye to all of them.

The plane ride home was just about four hours. I looked through bridal magazines I'd brought earlier, thinking about who I was going to ask to act as my maid of honor. Donna definitely would be my first choice. She and I had been friends since sixth grade. I would ask my sister Joyce if she wanted to be my maid of honor too. She would probably say something crazy when I ask her. She was highly upset at the whole family before I left. She was so mad at my mama and daddy for letting me go on this trip. I really didn't know how she would react to me getting married, but I really didn't care. The four-hour plane ride zoomed by. I had planned my whole wedding on the plane. I had decided that I would have six bridesmaids, two flower girls and a ring bearer. I loved to hear Kayla sing, so I was going to ask her to be the soloist. I wanted Cory to sing a duet with Kayla. Cory was my old boyfriend, Chris' best friend. We were all pretty cool and I was sure it would be fine with Cory and Chris. The only thing left to do was to call Bishop Jenkins when I got home.

My parents were at the airport to pick me up. I was so relieved that I had the ring on my finger to show my daddy

Thy Maker Is Thy Husband

because he wasn't going for any excuses or any crazy stuff. The first thing my mother said to me was, "Denise, let me see the ring."

"Ma, don't you want to give me hug or something first?" She said she just wanted to make sure everything was legitimate. I was talking a mile a minute, telling them all about California and how much I had enjoyed myself. I told my mama that Brian's sister Shirley was just like having a mother away from home. She would be looking in on us, so mama didn't have to worry. I knew my mom would be worried about me, living so far away, but she would be alright.

I was back on the home turf and had finished unpacking from my trip. I sat at the end of my bed and began to think about all of the things that had happened this past year. This time last year, getting married was probably on my mind as much as becoming a missionary. I thought about my relationship with the Lord as well. At this point in my life, I wasn't sure where I stood with the Lord. It had been a long time since I really felt the presence of God within me. I still went to church almost every Sunday. I read my Bible sometimes and prayed every night before I went to bed. But I was not going to lie to myself. I knew I was not where I used to be. I hoped when I called Bishop Jenkins in a few minutes, that he would give me his blessings. I remembered from Sunday school, the Scripture in *Proverbs 13:13* that reads: "Whoever despises the word and counsel of God brings destruction on himself, but he who fears and respects the commandment of God is rewarded." I knew that I was taking a big step and I had enough sense to go to my Pastor. Brian and I could have gotten married while I was in California, but we really wanted to try and do it right.

I was trying to get myself together to call the Bishop's house. You always had to be on your best when calling. You had to go through all the right motions. "Praise the Lord Sister Jenkins, this is Sister Denise Baker, Brother Martise's sister. Is Bishop Jenkins available?"

Gwendolyn Jackson

"Yes baby, hold the line just one minute. By the way, I haven't seen you in Sunday school lately."

"Yes Ma'am, I know. I will try to do better." Bishop Jenkins came to the phone, I was so nervous. "Praise the Lord Bishop Jenkins, this is Sister Denise Baker, Brother Martise's sister." That's how the Bishop identified everyone, by who they were related to.

"Praise the Lord daughter, what can I do for you?" I explained to the Bishop that Brian and I had been dating for several months and that he was a childhood friend and we had fallen in love and Brian had asked me to marry him. I told the Bishop that we would like it very much if he would give us his blessings and give us the honor of him marrying us. The Bishop started his one hundred question oral quiz. The Bishop's first question was; "Is this young man born again and filled with the Holy Ghost?" I told the Bishop that Brian was a Christian and he attended a Lutheran Church.

"I see." Bishop Jenkins proceeded to ask about Brian's parents. I explained that they were divorced and that Brian actually lived in California alone at the present time. The Bishop asked me a battery of questions and I felt like he did not like my responses. Finally, the Bishop said, "Okay daughter," then paused. I was thinking he meant okay he would marry us. Then he said, "NO daughter, the Lord is telling me to tell you no. Do not marry this man."

I said to the Bishop, "I don't understand, we love each other and everything is so perfect and right."

Bishop Jenkins immediately came with the scripture taken from *Proverbs 14:12*, "There is a way which seems right to a man and appears straight before him, but the end of it is the way to death." Bishop Jenkins read this to me twice. He was really starting to scare me. He then said, "Daughter, this is what the Lord has told me to tell you. But, it is up to you to make the right decision. I am telling you, if you do this, you are going to have trouble. I'm sorry Denise. I can't do it." As I cried, I told him that I understood and slammed the phone down.

Thy Maker Is Thy Husband

I screamed out loud, "Bishop Jenkins is tripping!!!!" I am going to marry Brian. We will get someone to marry us. When Brian called me, I was crying. I told him what Bishop Jenkins had said. He told me not to worry, that the Bishop was from the old school and didn't understand young people. I was so upset and tired that I couldn't think straight. I told Brian that I would call Grandpa Ned's pastor and ask him. It wouldn't be a problem, for I was quite sure that he would be the officiant at our wedding. Brian and I talked for three hours on the phone. We even prayed and asked the Lord to lead us the right way. We told God that we loved each other and we didn't understand why we couldn't be together. We were doing what the Bible said. Even God said marriage is honorable. We were not going to worry about it anymore after tonight. Brian and I decided to move forward with our plans and we were determined to have a beautiful wedding and live our lives together forever.

CHAPTER 2

I DO

It was a brand new year and I was excited about going back to school. Everybody who had told me that Brian was not serious about marrying me, well, today was the day I had to show everyone my engagement ring. Mrs. Franks, my Business Law teacher was so cool. I couldn't wait to see what she would say in first period today. "Hey Cynthia, girl I did it for real. Brian and I are officially engaged." As we were walking to class, Cynthia was looking at me with her mouth wide open.

"Denise, you are something else. I don't believe you. You have amazed me since I met you five years ago and you still continue to do so. Girl, my brother, Tommy was with Brian when he was here last year and Tommy said that Brian smoked weed, big time! And believe me, Tommy would know because he too smokes weed like it ain't no tomorrow. Denise, I don't want you to think that I am envious or anything, but you are a nice person and I would hate to see you get mixed up in a marriage to someone hooked on drugs."

I was getting more upset by the minute. I couldn't believe she would start off telling me some junk like that. I said to her, "Cynthia, why is it that every time a person wants to tell you something good, you always try to find something negative to say? You could have kept that to yourself for real. I know Brian smokes a little weed, but as far as being a weed head, that is a lie. I hate that I even said anything to you."

"Denise, you don't have to go off on me like that. I am not trying to hurt you. I am trying to show you that I care and just wanted you to know. Just forget I said anything. I wish you the best. Let me know if there is anything I can do."

I said, "Sure Cynthia, let's go to class."

All the girls in class crowded around my desk looking at my ring and asking about the wedding. Then all at once, Ms. Franks came in to the class. "Hey ladies, what's up? Is there something I need to see at Miss Baker's desk?"

Everyone said, "Ms. Franks, wait until you see this! Santa Claus was real good to Denise!"

"Let me see what Santa brought," Ms. Franks said. I stuck out my hand. "Did your little boyfriend give you your first promise ring?"

I said, "No Ma'am, I don't have a boyfriend, but a fiancée. This is not a promise ring, for I am getting married in June."

"Well la-te-da, girlfriend. All I have to say is that you are getting ready to buy you some sense. They always told me that bought sense is the best sense and I hope you can afford to pay the price. Bought sense is not cheap!"

"Ms. Franks, what was that supposed to mean?" She informed me that she had married a clown when she was twenty years old. And later found out that she could have done a whole lot better with her life had she waited until later. I told her she still turned out fine and I was sorry that she had gone to the circus to find a husband. I was trying to be funny. I told her I had gone to sunny California and had gotten a real man, not a clown. Ms. Franks reminded me not to forget what she had said to me.

After school that afternoon, Pam and I were walking up the street when Darnell's younger brother who was a freshman at O'Fallon, came running up the street behind me. The word had gotten around that I was getting married. He said, "Denise, why did you play my brother like that?"

"What are you talking about Lamont?"

"Girl, my brother is in love with you and you are getting married to Brian Turner. Darnell is so hurt." I told Lamont, "Darnell is not in love with me."

Lamont said, "I'm serious, I am not playing." I told him, oh well and would talk to him later. Pam and I couldn't believe that Darnell felt like that. I was really shocked.

I couldn't believe how fast the time was going. I had been so busy planning the wedding, preparing for graduation and completing that American History course three evenings a week, that April came before I knew it. It so happened that Darnell had to go to night school to take the same class in order to graduate. One evening, Darnell offered to give me a ride home from class. As we were driving down the street laughing and talking, I decided to ask him about what Lamont had said a few months ago. Darnell said that he had always cared for me.

Later that evening, Darnell called. He wanted to know if I would go to a movie and to dinner with him. Just to be on the safe side, I called Brian and asked if he would mind me going out with Darnell. He said he didn't mind at all. He told me to have a good time and to call him the next day. Darnell and I had a good time. We saw a good movie and ate pizza afterwards.

It was around 12:30 a.m. when we got back to my house. We sat in his car and listened to Shalimar and talked about our graduation and senior prom. One of those love songs by Shalimar came on and Darnell got real quiet. I asked him what was the matter. His eyes started to get teary and I was really getting concerned. When he finally said, "Denise, please don't get married. Don't leave me. I am in love with you and I want you to be with me. I know I am not ready for marriage or anything like that, but I know that someday I will marry you. Please don't leave me, don't marry him, I am begging you." I was so out done by what he was saying. I thought for a few minutes and I asked why he hadn't ever told me how he felt. Darnell told me that he was afraid of falling in love and that was why he would act silly with me all of the time. Darnell reached over to me and started hugging me and crying, I mean real crying. I started to cry too and I told Darnell it was too late for me to change my mind. I told him that my parents had spent a lot of money getting the hall and the caterer and the girls had already spent their money on the bridesmaid's dresses and it was just too late. Darnell hit his hand on the dashboard as hard as he could. As he walked me to my door with his head hanging low, he kissed me on the cheek and told me he would call me tomorrow. By the time I got in the house and got into bed, I just

Thy Maker Is Thy Husband

laid there. I didn't know what to do. I started to have second thoughts about all of this. Actually, I wanted to call it off, but I kept thinking of Brian and how it would hurt him if I didn't go through with it.

Over the next few weeks, Darnell and I spent a lot of time together and he finally accepted the fact that I was going to go through with the wedding. Darnell was the only person that knew I was having second thoughts about getting married. He told me it would be our little secret. I told Darnell that he would always be a very special person to me and I would never forget him. He was my very special friend.

Three weeks before the wedding, Reverend Thompson called to see if we would like to come in for marital counseling. I couldn't believe that it took him four months to call. I explained to him that my fiancée was still in California and would be here a week before the wedding. He told me to have Brian come talk to him an hour before the wedding. I knew it wasn't going to be as big a deal with the Reverend as it was with Bishop Jenkins. Grandpa Ned had been a member of his church for so long, he figured that if I came from his family, that the marriage would be just fine. I guessed he would counsel us at the altar.

As the wedding day approached, things got hectic around the house. I was trying to pack, get ready for graduation and the wedding. My soon to be mother-in-law and my mama went with me for the final fitting of my dress. Both of them saw me in it for the first time. They both just smiled and stared. Mrs. Williams said I looked like a princess. She told me that I was going to take Brian's breath away when he finally saw the dress. I wanted to look as beautiful as I could on our wedding day.

After five months, twenty-seven days and seven hours, I was finally going to pick up my future husband from the airport. My uncle Wardell had bought me a very nice Oldsmobile Cutlass for my graduation present. When Brian came through the gate, we hugged and kissed each other. We were so happy that our time had finally come. Later, we went to dinner to celebrate my birthday at a very nice restaurant. We talked about our last minute plans and our drive back to California after the wedding. Brian's buddy from Oakland was flying in to St. Louis in a couple of days to be in the wedding and to help us drive back to California. Brian calls him "Bush" all the time, but I finally found out that his name was Derek. Brian said he needed to go and talk to his future father-in-law. I asked Brian if he had invited his father. He said no, that he didn't want him to attend the wedding. He still had a lot of bad feelings towards his father from the past.

When we got back to my house, my father was laying in the den in his usual spot. "So you finally decided to come and talk to me. I was starting to wonder about you." Brian quickly responded. He said, "Sir, I wanted to talk to you face to face. I know you really don't know me that well and I came out of nowhere and now I am taking your baby girl clear across the country. I just wanted you to know that I am going to take good care of Denise." My father started asking him a lot of questions about his job and the area in which we would be living. When the conversation was just about over, my father said to Brian, "Well boy, you seem like you got a pretty good head on your shoulders, just don't get mixed up with them drugs out there in California. They tell me there's plenty of it out there. You don't use that stuff, do ya?" Brian said, "No Sir, I just drink a few beers every now and then." My father said, "O.K. boy. And don't drink too much beer either." My father went on to tell Brian that he could have my hand in marriage, but he would be watching. Brian laughed and gave my father a hug and was relieved he made it through the meeting.

After thirteen years of school, graduation day finally came. I ended up with a "B" in American History after taking it two times. I was so embarrassed about having to go to night school. My parents were also pretty disgusted about it, but that was over with now and the day of reckoning was here. It was so hard for me to get excited about graduation, since my wedding was the next day. I don't know why we didn't wait until the following

Thy Maker Is Thy Husband

weekend to get married. I guess I wanted all of my excitement at once. Graduating from high school one day and getting married and moving on to adulthood the next day. Brian and I went out and bought him a new suit for my graduation. It was too bad he wasn't walking across the stage with us. He ended up dropping out of school when he moved to California and got his GED.

It was a zoo at our house. All my relatives were in town for the wedding. My brother, sister and two cousins came from Memphis and there had to be at least fifteen people in the house. After graduation, I couldn't go out with the rest of my class because my wedding was to take place in less than twenty-four hours. The bridal party had to be at the salon at 6:00 a.m.; I hadn't even finished packing yet. Donna, my cousin, Rhonda, from Memphis and I were up until one in the morning trying to finish getting my things packed. I hoped and prayed that I didn't have bags under my eyes on my wedding day. When I finally laid down to sleep, I couldn't. I tossed and turned, getting very nervous about the next day. I thought about Bishop Jenkins' refusal to marry us because he felt it wasn't time and Brian wasn't the right person for me. I thought about Darnell's confession of love; just so many things were running through my head. I got out of bed and got on my knees and said this prayer: "Dear Lord, tomorrow I have decided to take a very big step in my life. Over the past few months, I have had a lot of mixed feelings about the whole situation and I don't even understand what I am feeling sometimes. Bishop Jenkins told me that you said for me not to marry Brian. Lord, I am doing what you said in your Word, that it is better to marry than to burn. So Lord, I am asking you to do this one thing for me, if this is not your will for my life, please show me a sign. Amen." I went ahead and drifted off to sleep from there.

It was my wedding day and I couldn't believe that this was real. I looked pretty good for having just a few hours of sleep. Brian called me that morning to see if I still loved him and wanted to be his wife. In a quiet soft voice, I said, "Yes, Brian, I love you and I am happy that I am going to be your wife in about five hours and would see him at the altar."

Everything was running smoothly. No one seemed to be late or anything. I called the hall where the reception was to be held and things were going as planned. The flowers had arrived and the church was decorated. Kayla and Cory had arrived a little early, practicing their duet. I was looking out of the window where I was getting dressed and saw the guests as they were going into the church. Darnell came just like he promised. I was so shocked. Even Chris showed up. You would have thought that we were celebrities, for there were so many people there. I guess this was the royal wedding of St. Louis. My Aunt Rita came to do my makeup. She's the fashion expert of the family. When she finished, I looked like a million bucks. The only thing left to do was to slip into my dress. Donna was more nervous than I was. She ripped her pantyhose and then she lost Brian's ring under the bed in the dressing room. Donna looked so beautiful as my maid of honor. She and the bridesmaids wore powder blue chiffon dresses that were so wide I wasn't sure how they were going to sit at the table during the reception. My sister Joyce decided that she would be a hostess and work at the gift table.

It was time for me to take that walk down the aisle of no return. I got so nervous seeing all those people in the church that my face began to tremble and my hands shook. I held my composure so that no one could tell that I was nervous. Camera lights were flashing in every direction and it seemed like it took forever to get to the altar. As I was nearing the front of the church, Brian stared at me in complete awe. He took my hand and we began to repeat our vows. After meeting Brian at age nine, barely speaking in high school, meeting again by a mere chance of fate, the moment had finally come. I felt like I had drifted off into another place in time and then snapped back into reality when Reverend Thompson said, "By the power invested in me by the Lord and Savior Jesus Christ and the State of Missouri, I pronounce you husband and wife. I couldn't believe

Thy Maker Is Thy Husband

it. We had done it. I was finally Mrs. Denise Baker Turner. Brian took me in his arms and kissed me in the most loving, passionate way. Outside, in front of the church, was a white limousine waiting to charter me "Cinderella" and Brian the "Prince" to our reception.

By the time we arrived at the reception, everything was in high gear. I was exhausted, but I had to keep smiling. We still had to greet our guests. I kept starring at Brian. I couldn't believe I now had a husband. We hugged and kissed every bit of three hundred or so people that afternoon. Finally, we got to sit down. Brian had disappeared for a long time and finally, he came back. He was as high as a kite. I asked him what he had been doing. He had drunk a whole bottle of champagne and smoked a joint. I told him that I hated that weed smoking and I wished he would stop. He said this is his wedding day and he was going to celebrate and not to worry. Brian and I both went our separate ways, greeting our guests. I went to talk to Darnell. I gave him a big hug, we took a picture together and I told him thanks for being such a good friend to me and for sharing in my special day. I will never forget Darnell and will always wonder if I should have listened to him.

The wedding reception was winding down, everyone had a good time and Brian and I were heading off to our honeymoon suite. As we were driving down the highway, the strangest thing overcame me. It was weirdest thing I had ever felt. I didn't say anything to Brian, but I couldn't erase it. When we arrived at the hotel, the staff greeted us like royalty. Brian picked me up and carried me over the threshold of our room and we fell on to the bed. Both of us were worn out, but we weren't too tired to count the money in our money gift box. We were rolling in the bed with excitement at seeing all of the hundred and fifty dollar bills. When we had counted all of the money, the total amounted to almost two thousand dollars. I couldn't believe on my wedding day, that mother- nature had come to visit me. I thought to myself, "Is God trying to tell me something?" By seven o'clock, we both were asleep. That was our honeymoon night. Lots of fun! NOT!

The next day was a bittersweet day. I knew it would be my last day at home and the day after that, I would be moving two thousand miles away. I had to love Brian a lot to move that far away from my family. I felt he would take excellent care of me. I also felt a sense of security with his older sister living near us in California. Brian and I went around visiting as Mr. and Mrs. Brian Turner. The family was giving us their blessings and advice for newlyweds. We listened and smiled as they talked to us, telling us all of their war stories. I tell you, it seemed like all of the older people always had these sad old stories about how rough things get down the marriage road. Brian and I told our family that we hated to hear that things were rough for them, but that our love was as solid as a rock and we didn't plan on seeing that side of the road. My daddy said to us to just live a while.

I had a chance to talk to my brother, Martise, before we left. He was the only one that I told about that strange feeling that had previously overcome me as Brian and I drove down the highway. Martise was sort of like my spiritual mentor and I figured he may have had an answer. He said that the Lord could have been doing something in the spirit.

I said, "Doing something like what?"

He said, "Maybe removing the hedge from around you."

"Why would you say that?"

"You asked me what I thought and I am telling you. Remember what the Word says? "There is a way which seemeth right unto a man, but the end thereof are the ways of death" *Proverbs 14:12, KJV.*

I didn't tell Martise, but that was the same thing Bishop Jenkins had said to me. I said to myself, "Oh God, what have I done?"

The sun was starting to set and I went out and sat on the front porch. Brian's best friend Curtis came out on the porch with me. He saw that I was kind of sad and he said to me, "Denise don't worry, Brian is going to take care of you. He loves you very much. I know it." I told Curtis that I believed that Brian loved me and I felt he would do his best to take care of me, but I was worried about the weed smoking and drinking. Curtis said that Brian had good self-control and that he wouldn't over do it. Curtis hugged me and told me to cheer up.

All of my friends came by to tell me goodbye- Donna, Cynthia and Pam. They were all crying, telling me to take care of my new husband and myself. I promised them all that I would keep in touch. I was really going to miss Donna. She and I were like sisters. She was going to have to take my place working at the store. I know she was thrilled about that! NOT! But that would keep her close to the family and she would get her weekend sausage and egg sandwiches from her Nunie.

After everyone had left, Brian came out on the porch. He took my hand said, "Denise, I love you and I want you to know that I am not going to take you two thousand miles away from home and not take care of you. Denise, you are my life and I will protect you and take care of you for the rest of my life." I told him thank you. I felt more confident about moving to California than ever before. I was ready. Brian and I went into the house and slept in the same bed in my parents' home for the first time as husband and wife.

CHAPTER 3

MARRIAGE – 101

The alarm clock went off at 6:00 a.m. This was it. I was taking the final big plunge into the real world today. Mama and daddy were preparing to see their baby girl move thousands of miles away with someone they hardly knew. My mama had some sense of comfort knowing that Brian's older sister, Shirley would just be a few miles away from us. Still, it was hard for her to see me leave. She just felt that I had made this decision too fast and I should have finished college before deciding to get married.

Brian and his friend Bush had packed the car and checked everything over before our journey to California. It was finally time to say goodbye to all of my friends and loved ones. The thing I had wished for was that I could take my mama and daddy with me. They are my friends. But, I guess you can't have it all at once in life. I still couldn't believe that I was Mrs. Denise Turner. We hugged and kissed everyone before getting into the car. As we pulled off down the street, I waved goodbye. I felt very happy and sad at the same time. As we headed down Highway I-44 west towards California, Brian turned towards me and started singing "A Ribbon in the Sky" by Stevie Wonder. Bush said to Brian, "Man, don't tell me you and your wife are going to sing love songs to each other for the next twenty-six hours in this car!"

I know Bishop Jenkins is a man of God, but maybe he missed it on this one, because he is still a human being and can make mistakes. If he had only had a chance to meet Brian, maybe, he would have thought differently about our marriage. I was so happy we were beginning a wonderful life together. I had to follow my heart and see where this road would lead us. If nothing else, I could say that I wasn't afraid to take chances and maybe I should have been. Once, I had heard that most of the millionaires in this country became successful because they were great risk takers. Most of them failed two or three times before they succeeded. If they had been afraid to take chances, they wouldn't be who they are today. Like those millionaires, I would have to step out and take a chance too. The first step was made when we said until death do us part and all I could do was pray that we could keep the vows that we had promised each other.

Brian had just started his turn driving, when we were pulled over by the highway trooper. We were in a part of Missouri where they had a reputation of not being very nice to African-Americans. The trooper came up to the car and said a few choice words to Brian. Brian was driving thirty miles over the speed limit and we were required to pay a one hundred-dollar fine on the spot, be stranded, or go to jail. We got pass that ordeal and didn't let it spoil our happiness. Brian and Bush took turns driving for the rest of the day, before we were forced to stop. There were terrible storms in and all around Texas. I wasn't afraid at all, being with Brian, I felt so safe. Normally, when the weather services issued tornado warnings and sirens rang, I got very sick to my stomach and my palms would sweat. I believed so much that Brian was going to protect me, even from the tornadoes.

We started the next leg of our journey right before sunrise. Brian and Bush were determined to get across the Oakland Bay Bridge that night. I had to get a lot of cushion for my bottom because I had twenty hours of riding to endure.

The sun was rising as we crossed the New Mexico border. I had never seen anything so beautiful in all my life. Even though I wasn't serving God the way I once had, I still realized how amazing and awesome He was. I mean this was absolutely gorgeous. The air was so clean and clear. For years I'd had allergy problems. But when we stepped out of the car in New Mexico, it seemed like the air went all the way to my brain! It was great! I got so excited from all of the beauty that I ran to a pay phone to call my mama to tell her where we were and how beautiful the view was. I could tell in her voice that she was happy to hear that we had made it that far. The first thing my mother asked was, "Brian isn't speeding is he?"

I said, "Ugh, no ma'am, he's driving just fine."

We got back into the car and continued our journey. Before I knew it, we were crossing the Mojave Desert in Arizona. Brian and Bush were driving 90 to 100 mph in the desert. Bush was a professional truck driver, so he was used to driving across the desert. When it was Brian's turn, guess what, right out in the middle of the desert, a state trooper appeared again. He received another traffic ticket and this time it was one hundred and fifty dollars. We didn't care. We just paid it out of the money we had received as part of our wedding gifts. We were two young people with almost two thousand dollars in cash. We didn't feel that we had a worry in the world.

After that incident, I went ahead and took my nap while Brian drove. I awakened to the smell of marijuana. I didn't let him know that I was awake at first. I just lay there and watched them. Bush was rolling up another joint for them to smoke and this time, he sprinkled what appeared to be cocaine in the joint with the marijuana. I sat straight up in my seat and said, "What in the hell is going on?" Brian was startled when I started yelling right in front of Bush. I told him that I was not going to ride down the highway with anybody doing cocaine and smoking dope. I went on to tell him that he knew how I felt about smoking weed. But that I refused to put up with anything that had to do with cocaine. I was so upset with Brian.

We finally stopped at a McDonald's as we were coming near a town in the desert. Brian pulled over and told me to get out of the car so that we could talk. At first, I refused, but as he continued to gently persuade me, I went ahead and listened. Brian's excuse was that he needed to stay awake. He said he was really tired and needed something to keep him alert. I didn't buy that excuse for one minute. I told him he should have drunk coffee or tea like normal people do when they need to stay awake. Bush stayed over by the car and looked unconcerned.

Thy Maker Is Thy Husband

As I started walking towards the car, Brian begged me not to say anything to him. But I didn't care; I was going to tell him a thing or two. I walked up to Bush and told him, "I don't appreciate you disrespecting me in my car, smoking drugs. We all could have gone to jail when we were pulled over twice by the state troopers." Before I could finish, Brian walked over and they both apologized. Brian told me that he would not smoke anything else for the rest of the trip. I sat in the front seat with Brian as we crossed the California State line. I was still fuming. I started thinking about the conversation that Bishop Jenkins and I had. Over and over in my mind, I kept hearing his voice saying, "the Lord said don't do it daughter, you're going to have troubles." I really wanted to ignore it, but I couldn't because the drug issue had been discussed on several different occasions and I just wanted to believe that it was not going to cause problems in our lives.

My ears started to hurt as we drove through the mountains. I took a cap full of nighttime cold medicine and went to sleep for the next eight hours. Brian woke me up and said, "Denise baby, we are home. We are crossing the Oakland Bay Bridge." I couldn't believe that we had made it to California in a day and a half. We started heading down Highway 101 to my new home in Redwood City, California. Brian had rented a one-bedroom apartment in Redwood City, across the street from his job. We didn't have bedroom furniture, so the remainder of our honeymoon would be spent on the sofa bed and that was fine with me. I was with the one that I loved and that was all that mattered to me.

On my first full day in my new home, Brian took me around the town. He made sure I was able to find all of my favorite places such as the mall and the grocery store for starters. We opened our first bank account together as Mr. and Mrs. Turner. All of these new things were exciting for me. Brian's brother, Richard and his wife, Faye, from St. Louis, were our next door neighbors. I was happy to have a hometown girl close by. Faye was really funny and I found out quickly that she didn't take any crap from Richard. I was so happy and excited at being in my new home and wanted to get things situated. I was in our bedroom one day unpacking some of my winter clothes when I noticed that some of my sweaters and one of my coats were missing. A sickening feeling came over me. I went to the other room and told Brian that someone had stolen some of my clothes and a piece of luggage that I had left when I had last visited. I asked Brian what type of people would he let into the apartment that would steal my clothes? Brian claimed that it was probably his roommate and a woman that he had there sometimes. We went over to Richard's apartment and told him what had happened. No one had a clue as to what had happened to the clothes. I wanted to call the police, but Richard and Brian didn't want me to. My first week in California and I was a victim of a robbery. That made me begin to wonder about the people around me. Brian told me not to worry about my things. He would buy me some more sweaters and a new coat.

Fridays were payday for both Brian and me. Fortunately, I was blessed to get a job at Prudential Insurance Company as a mail clerk. We were so proud. Both of us had take home paychecks of two hundred dollars a week. We were living high on the hog. The only bills we had were our rent, utilities and car insurance. We lived for the weekend. I saw myself beginning to compromise on Brian's weed smoking.

On payday, Brian would go around the corner and buy ten dollars worth of weed from this old Asian lady that was seventy years old. Brian referred to her as "Granny," the dope lady. Brian would refer to the weed as being "fire," meaning that it was good stuff. Brian got back into the car with the weed. It smelled sort of good, almost like pine trees. He said that the name of the weed was "Ses." He rolled a joint in the car and we cruised down Highway 101 to the city. Brian asked me if I wanted to hit the joint, at first I said no, but then, I changed my mind. It wasn't bad at all - actually, it was pretty good. It made me feel very relaxed. When Brian and I would go to the city, we would always go to the arcade to play Ms. Pac Man and it

Thy Maker Is Thy Husband

seemed like we played really well after smoking a joint. My husband told me that if one is going to get high, it's best to do it with someone you love. I thought it was so much fun that when we got back home, I wanted to do it again. We had more fun in our honeymoon suite that night, – if you know what I mean!

We were starting to settle into our married life. I began to miss going to church and told Brian that I wanted to go. His sister, Shirley, went to church in the city and I went with her. It was nice, but it wasn't what I was used to. I wanted to go to church with my husband, but Brian didn't want to go. We started to get into little arguments about it. Brian would say that I knew he wasn't a church going man when I married him, so I shouldn't try to make him something that he didn't want to do. What he said was true. I did know that before we got married, but I guess deep down inside, I was hoping that we could still serve God together in some form or another. I felt my life drifting further and further away from God. It was as though I had made a choice between Brian and the Lord and I chose Brian.

Time had gone by so quickly since we were married. It was already September. My sister, Joyce had come to visit. I was happy that she had come, for I knew that she was against my marriage. Joyce stayed with us for a week. We took her every where in the San Francisco Bay Area. She had a blast. My sister-in-law and sister had become inseparable. Joyce's visit went by so quickly, that I was sad to see her leave. I really wished she could have stayed, even though she could be pretty hateful. She was still my big sister and I knew she loved me, but had a strange way of showing it.

Married life with Brian was pretty sweet. I started enjoying smoking weed. It got so bad that I couldn't make love to my husband unless we had smoked a joint. I knew it would eventually turn into a big problem for us, so I decided that I was going to stop getting high with him before things got out of hand. I never liked anything controlling me.

Gwendolyn Jackson

One night before we went to bed, I told Brian that I didn't want to get high anymore and explained the reason why. I told him that I didn't want to be high on drugs to be able to fulfill my wifely duties and furthermore, I was too strong willed to let anything like that control my mind, moods and emotions.

Brian and I had started talking about moving back to St. Louis. We always thought we would stay in California, raise our children there and make a life for ourselves and maybe one day, open up a convenience store. But with the holidays approaching, I began to get homesick. I started to miss my family and friends. Finally, I just told Brian that I wanted to move back home. My sweet husband said to me, "Whatever makes you happy, baby, I will do for you." I was so happy that Brian was very understanding. In my heart, I knew that I wanted to go back home, but I hated to leave Shirley. We had become very close and I knew that if we left, it would break her heart. Mrs. Williams, Brian's mother was very upset when she got news that we were thinking of moving back home. She felt that being away from home was the best thing for him and that we would only have trouble if we came home. I didn't understand why she felt that way and I really wasn't too concerned. It was a hard decision to make, but we decided to move. And of course, it made my mother very happy.

We tried our best to return to St. Louis for Thanksgiving, but ended up having to eat Thanksgiving Dinner at Denny's in California. I began to understand the importance of family during the holidays. It was a sad day in a way, but I knew that we would be home soon. Both Brian and I had job leads in St. Louis. The only thing we could do was hope and pray that our marriage would continue to grow stronger and our love for one another would grow deeper no matter where we lived.

CHAPTER 4

ABOARD A SINKING SHIP

It had been more than a year since Brian and I had been back in St. Louis. Things hadn't worked out for me at the insurance company where I had worked. I was able to get a new job in patient accounts in one of the hospitals in St. Louis. Meanwhile, Brian had been unemployed for the past ten months. Today, he had an interview with one of the airlines, working in the food service department.

I hadn't gotten up enough nerve to tell Brian that I had missed my period last month. So it would probably freak him out if I told him that "I might" be pregnant and he didn't have a job.

After ten months of unemployment, Brian got a new job with an airline. I took a home pregnancy test the same day to confirm that Brian I were going to have our first child. When Brian got home, I told him. He was very excited and I was relieved. Brian sat me down and said, "Denise, I know things have not worked out these last few months like we had planned and I know that it has been hard on you trying to make ends meet by yourself. I am going to take this burden off you, be the man and take care of my family." I told him that I believed that he was going to do exactly what he said. We were so excited about the baby. We went out to celebrate Brian's new job and the new baby on the way. I really hoped it was a boy.

After meeting a guy that Brian worked with, Brian finally agreed to start going to church sometimes. Brian's coworker attended Living Word Church of God. Brian and I got together on Sunday's with he and his wife to attend church with them. Brian and his friend cracked me up, they would go to church and get all into the service like they were really living the Christian life, then they would fire up a joint before we could get home good.

Gwendolyn Jackson

Time was moving on. The baby was due in November and Brian's job at the airline allowed us to fly practically free of charge. We could fly to California for fifteen dollars. We decided to go and visit Shirley for a weekend. I didn't know how much fun I would have being pregnant and all, but I was hardly ever sick. So I figured that I would be fine. We were excited about going back to our old stomping ground. When we arrived in the Bay area, things still looked the same.

After we got settled, the first thing Brian wanted to do was go buy some weed. I started thinking to myself. "He is really a weed head." I just sat there and didn't say a word. I started thinking about some of the stuff Martise and Bishop Jenkins had said to me. I decided to try and have a nice visit with my in-laws and deal with my family problems later.

Brian and I had to leave early to get back to St. Louis so that he could get back to work. I really hated that we had to leave so fast. Three days was not long enough to be in California, but it was nice anyway. This was the third trip we had taken this year. We were trying to get all our trips in before the baby came.

It had been a very long and hot summer. A lot of things had happened that year. Marvin Gaye's father was charged with his murder; over two hundred marines had been killed by suicide terrorists in the Middle East. I got scared sometimes, just thinking about bringing a child into all the crazy madness that was going on, but I guess we couldn't quit living. Brian was very good about going with me to my doctor's appointments during my pregnancy. He hadn't missed one. He seemed very excited about having a baby. This was his first child. So many young guys had two or three babies by the time they were twenty-one.

However, Brian and I had not been getting along like we used to. He didn't seem as excited about our marriage and relationship anymore. Brian would rather go play basketball than to take a ride to the park with me. When we lived in California, almost every Sunday afternoon, we would ride down Pacific Highway One. Now that we were back in St. Louis, we

Thy Maker Is Thy Husband

were starting to drift apart. Maybe things would get better when the baby came.

Sometimes, I felt that Brian didn't tell the truth. He always used the excuse that flights were late and that he had to work overtime to service the airplanes. I guess he thought I was stupid. That I wouldn't approve of what he was doing if he told me. I know Brian liked hanging out with the fellows and getting high after work. He smoked weed so much now, that I don't think it even made him high anymore. It was just like a cigarette to him. Those days, I found myself wondering what I would have been doing if I hadn't married Brian. I wondered if I would have been back on track with God, or how I would have been doing in college had gone on to Washington University or some other school. But I guess none of that really mattered. I was a married young woman with a baby on the way.

On my due date, labor kicked in. Brian and Mrs. Williams were hilarious. He kept going into the bathroom because he couldn't stand seeing me in pain and his mother was hollering, telling him to get out of the bathroom and come help deliver the baby. My mom had left the hospital many hours ago. The next thing I knew, they were rolling me down the hall to the delivery room and Brian got all ready to help out. I pushed a couple of times and our baby son was born; Brian Christopher Turner. The baby was fine. I was in shock when Brian left right after his birth. I was really hurt because he had hardly spent an hour with us.

When I got home, the house was a mess. I couldn't believe it. Dishes were in the sink and the bed hadn't been made up. Then one of my girlfriends called me to say that she had seen Brian kicking it at a club. I couldn't wait to ask Brian about this. I am lying up in the hospital and he is out partying. I guess he couldn't wait for me to have the baby so that he could be a single man for a few days. When he got home, I asked him about it and he told me that he was out celebrating the birth of his son. Further more, he is grown and didn't have to explain anything to me. I couldn't believe he had said that, but if he wanted to go off on me like that, then I definitely had to come back with something. We argued. Brian started cursing and left. I just fell to my knees and asked God why things had been so difficult. Sure enough, God answered me. It came to me through a form of scripture: ***"The way of the transgressor is hard," Proverbs 13:15.*** I thought to myself, boy, I have really lost my connection with the Lord. He told me, this was what I got because I had chosen not to listen to the counsel I had received from Bishop Jenkins.

As little Brian's first Christmas neared, things between Brian and me were getting a little better. He was spending a lot of time with the baby and me. He cooked dinner, cleaned the house and helped a lot with the baby. It seemed as though things would be all right after all. We didn't have a lot of money this Christmas, but it still was pretty nice. We spent time with the family and we took little Brian to visit all of his relatives.

A couple of days after Christmas, Brian and I got into a huge fight. We fought over money. Brian's insurance paid my medical bills even though he didn't work for the airlines anymore. That was one thing I did remember from Prudential, that if I were totally disabled at the time the insurance was terminated, the bills would still be paid. Anyway, a check for over $400 for the doctor's bill came to the house. Brian took the check and cashed it and didn't pay the bill. I told him that it was shameful to keep the money. He went completely off on me and I told him I was leaving and going home. I packed all my stuff and took the baby with me.

On New Year's Eve, my friend, Mamie, called to see if I would go to church with her. I didn't know what was happening to me. I said to myself, "What if some of the old "saints" started asking me questions and they find out that I have turned away from the Lord? What will they say?" Then out of the blue, Keena, another friend called to see if I wanted to go to the East Side to a club. I was very curious, so I told her yes. For the first time in a long time, I felt the Lord pulling at my heart. I knew I should have gone to church and that God had something special for me, but I was just too ashamed.

New Year's Day 1985 had come and gone and Brian and I were still separated. It had been a week since I had left. I was starting to miss him. I was sleepy from staying out all night with Keena, but I couldn't rest until I had spoken to Brian, but I was too stubborn to call him. When he finally called, he said to me, "Denise, Happy New Year, I love you, baby and I want you to come home today." We talked for sometime on the phone and I told Brian that I was tired of working by myself, trying to pay the bills with him getting high all of the time. He told me that he would stop smoking weed and that he would try hard to find a job. I decided to go back home, to try again. I told Brian how I went to the club the other night instead of going to church with Mamie. Brian didn't see anything wrong with me going to the club. I said to him that I was always in church during my teenage years and going to parties and stuff had never been my thing. I told him I hadn't been truly happy in my life since then. I just broke down and told him how much I wanted my relationship with God back and how that could help our marriage. I also wanted us to seek the Lord together. I went and got the Bible and showed him a scripture in *II Corinthians 6:14*: "Be ye not unequally yoked together with unbelievers; for what fellowship hath righteousness with unrighteousness? And what communion hath light with darkness?" Brian looked at me like I was crazy and told me to go somewhere with that mess.

Brian was not at his new job a good two weeks, when he began to change. He got the "big head" big time!! He thought he was lifestyles of the rich and famous. He barely wanted to spend time at home. He always had something going on with the new job. All of the promises that he had made at the beginning of the year had flown out of the window. It was hard to believe that this person that I had shared so many happy times with was turning into someone that I understood less and we were growing father apart each day.

Gwendolyn Jackson

One day, Brian told me that I paid more attention to little Brian than I did to him. He said that he was in my life first. I thought that was a pretty silly statement for him to make. What did he expect, for the baby to take care of himself? I didn't care what he thought at that point. I felt let down and all of the dreams that we had seemed to slowly fade. In just the first six months of this year, we had separated at least three times.

We were going to have about fifty people over for Little Brian's first birthday. Brian was out as usual and I thought I would do some extra cleaning since all the family was coming over. I decided that I would clean out the pantry in the kitchen from top to bottom. Way back in the back, I found a bag I didn't remember putting there. I opened the bag and couldn't believe what I saw. A brown glass smoking pipe, a part of a clothes hanger, cotton balls and a small bag of white powdery substance, which appeared to be cocaine were in the bag. I had never seen cocaine in person before, but from what I had seen on TV and in the movies, that is what it looked like to me.

I was devastated! I knew something was going on with Brian, but I wasn't sure what it was. I knew he wasn't paying the bills like he should. He would always pretend that he was short two and three hundred dollars a week because he had a washer and dryer or new wedding rings in lay-a-way for Christmas. This started to happen every other week or so and none of this stuff ever made it home. The weed smoking was bad enough, but cocaine! I heard that that stuff was so addictive, it could drive people crazy. The experts said that when you smoked it in the pipe, it was even worse. Cocaine smoked, snorted, shot, or whatever, I couldn't believe this was happening to us!

I heard Brian's keys at the door and I didn't even let him get in the door. I ran and opened it and said to him, "Brian! No! Please tell me no! You are not using cocaine! I found this bag with all of this stuff in the kitchen pantry. What is this? Whose is it? Brian, I won't be able to take it, you are doing cocaine. Why, Brian, why?"

Thy Maker Is Thy Husband

Brian replied by saying, "Denise, there's a lot of pressure out there on the job; drugs and alcohol all over the place. One day after work, the fellas got together and they had a little cocaine and I smoked some with them. Since then, I have been using it. I am not out of control with it and I am not addicted. I do it just to be social at times and to relax."

I was so upset that I pushed him and started screaming, "I should never have married you, you drug addict!" Brian told me to quit tripping and to calm down. He tried to change the story after he saw how I had reacted and said that he was just kidding. He said that stuff in the bag was his cousin Nathan's. I didn't believe it for one minute. He claimed that he just wanted to see how I would react if he said it was his. From that day on, I knew what I was dealing with. A husband on cocaine! I hoped and prayed that I had enough strength to make it through this. I could hardly believe anything Brian told me. Shortly after this incident, the baby and I came home one day, the front door was unlocked, Brian's uniform was lying on the sofa and the kitchen doors were wide open. I thought someone had broken into the house and hurt him. Come to find out later that he was out kicking it with his homies and didn't even go to work. Things were starting to get out of control.

A couple of nights ago, Brian had stayed out the entire night. Although I wanted revenge, I knew I would hurt myself and destroy everything that I once stood for. Cynthia and I made a plan. She told her boyfriend that she was going out with me and I told Brian that I was going out with Cynthia. Actually, this guy on my job with whom I had become good friends and I were going out. I knew that Brian had begun to see other women in addition to doing serious drugs. So I proceeded to go and meet my friend. I committed what I considered the ultimate sin. I cheated on my husband. I couldn't believe I did it myself. I was going deeper and deeper into the pit. I also ruined a very good friendship. I tried to justify what I had done all the way home. Nothing I told myself gave me comfort. I rushed into the house and took a long hot shower, thinking it would wash away what I had done; that I would feel clean and everything would be all right. The shower didn't help.

What I didn't realize was that I was dirty on the inside and only God could make a difference. I laid there in bed waiting and listening for Brian to come home, hoping and praying that he wouldn't want to be romantic or anything tonight of all nights. I shouldn't have been worried at all, because it rarely happened much anymore. I had tears rolling down my face wetting my pillow and I prayed this prayer: "Dear Lord, I know I am not living for you right now, but what I did tonight was really bad. I made a big mistake going out on my husband. Lord, please forgive me for doing this, please Lord. I promise never to do this again. I know that I shouldn't have done this just to get even. I violated my wedding vows. So Lord, please help me and forgive me for this. Amen."

A few minutes later, I heard Brian coming up the stairs. He was very humble and kind, tonight of all nights. He leaned over in bed and kissed me and asked how my night out with Cynthia was. I told him it was O.K. He wanted to know every detail. I had to tell one lie after another because of what I had done. I just had to play the game like everyone else did. I found out that night that this could turn into a very dangerous game. I asked myself, lying in bed that night, "Are you so lonely, empty and frustrated with your marriage and your life that you have allowed yourself to go out like that?" I felt that I had gotten pretty pathetic. But nothing could change what had happened.

Our marriage had grown even worse. I found out that Brian was messing around with a woman on his job. After work one night, Joyce, Cynthia and I met at the house with one of my father's friends who had a truck. I was sick and tired of this mess. I cleaned out the entire house in a matter of hours. By the time we had finished, there was nothing left but a pot and a television set. I wanted to be a fly on the wall to see his face when he walked in the house that night. He had treated me like dirt, so I was giving him back what he deserved. He didn't need a wife nor did he deserve to have a family. I gave Brian just what he wanted – FREEDOM!!

Of course, I let him sucker me back into coming home after a week or two. I probably went back and forth a half dozen times over the next two years. One would begin to wonder how much more I could take before I went over the edge. I just wanted to believe that things would eventually change, but this marriage may have been cursed from the very beginning.

CHAPTER 5

A HOUSE DIVIDED

My twenty-second birthday was a few days away. Nathan moved in with us. Nathan was Brian's dope smoking companion, as well as his cousin. I always felt that Nathan was a very bad influence on Brian and contributed to him getting more addicted on that crap. Some days when Brian was at work I wouldn't even let him in the house. We barely spoke. Those drugs got his mind too. He didn't take care of himself at all. Two psychopaths surrounded my son and me. I figured you had to be weak and sick in your mind already to do that to yourself.

The stress from my life was beginning to take a toll on me. Over the past two months, I had lost over fifteen pounds and was continuing to lose weight. I cried everyday and had a terrible rash all over my body. This pus like substance was oozing from my breasts. I smoked over a pack of cigarettes a day. I was really messed up. I felt like I was on the very brink of losing it myself. The only thing that kept me sane was my son. If it hadn't been for him, I wouldn't have had anything to live for. I had made a complete mess of my life. And it all went back to the warning Bishop Jenkins had given me. Bishop Jenkins had told me that the Lord said for me not to marry this man, but I didn't listen. I did what I wanted and was paying dearly for it. The price that I paid for being disobedient to God was so severe that I didn't think I would make it. I picked up my Bible, barely remembering any of the scriptures that I had learned. I did though remember this verse from ***Psalms 51:10*** that reads; ***"Create in me a clean heart, O God; and renew a right spirit within me."*** I will never forget that day. I fell on my knees and began sobbing and crying out to the Lord. I told him I was so sorry for disobeying him and wanted him in my life again. I was so tired of living in misery and only He could make things right.

Thy Maker Is Thy Husband

I don't think I had ever prayed like that before. I felt release inside. I knew God had heard me and He was going to help me.

Things with Brian grew worse. He began staying out all night with other women. I thought I had finished going through changes with him after I had prayed. But I guess Satan wasn't finished throwing punches at me. I thought it was time I called my mother-in-law, Mrs. Williams to let her know what had been going on. I normally did not involve our family members in our problems, but I thought it was time.

When I called his mother and began telling her what had been happening between Brian and me, she patiently listened. Then in a laughing, joking tone, she said, "Denise, Brian ain't doing no cocaine. He may smoke that weed, but I can't believe he is doing that mess!" I was so upset with her, I couldn't understand why she would think I would call her and say that her son was using cocaine when it wasn't true. I told her that he was fooling everyone and one day, she would see that I had been telling the truth. I hung up in complete disgust. The next morning when Brian strolled into the house, I pretended to go about my normal routine and ignore the fact that it was ten o'clock, Saturday morning and he was just coming home. He walked in and looked at me without saying anything. I continued doing my housework as if I hadn't seen him. Suddenly, he walked up and got right in my face and said, "Denise you know I really hate you. I am going to make you so sick and tired of me that you will have to leave." I was stunned that he would even say anything like that to me. I knew we had grown apart and didn't have much of a relationship left, but I didn't think he had grown to hate me. I kept asking myself what I had done to make him feel that way. I realized then that the women, the money and the drugs had turned him into a different person. I was so hurt and shocked. Brian continued the verbal abuse, following me from one room to the next. He saw that I was really hurting, but it didn't matter to him. Later that same day, I was in the kitchen and he walked up behind me and whispered in my ear, "Denise, I am going to drive you out of here." He had pushed me to the limit. I turned around and grabbed a knife out of the dish rack and pushed him up against the refrigerator and told him that I would kill him. I told Brian how he had ruined my life and how marrying him had caused my relationship with God to go straight to hell. I also told him that if he so much as sneezed, his life would be over. I was a mess. He had pushed me as far as I could go.

By this time, Nathan had come up from the basement. He grabbed me and told me to put the knife down. He then turned to Brian and told him to leave me alone. He said, "Brian man, she was in here minding her own business and you came in here starting something with her." Brian started cursing Nathan, telling him to mind his own business. Nathan told Brian that he was making this his business. I went to grab the phone to call the police and Brian snatched it from the wall. I ran to the front door to go next door, struggling with him trying to get out. I finally bit him and got away to call. I ran three doors to the neighbor's with little Brian in my arms. When the police arrived, I told them what had happened. They told him to get his things and not to return to the residence until further notice. I couldn't believe that Nathan had stood up for me like that. I had not been nice to him at all, but I really appreciated what he had done for me. I guess blood isn't always thicker than water!

After we all calmed down, I called my parents and they came right over. My daddy changed the locks on the doors. I just knew I would hear those famous words, "I told you so!" But I didn't. I guess they figured I didn't need to hear that then. Later that night, I talked to Nathan and told him that I was sorry for being so mean to him, but I had always felt he was the cause of Brian's drug dependency. He told me that he could see where I was coming from, so I didn't have to worry about what had happened in the past. Nathan said he had to do what he thought was right.

Kayla called me the next morning. I hadn't spoken to her in a very long time. I guess I avoided talking to her because I always thought that she was going to ask me about my coming

Thy Maker Is Thy Husband

back to church. She asked me every now and then, why I was running from my God-given calling. I'd been thinking about that quite often. Kayla invited me to church that afternoon. There was some sort of convention in town and she was going to be there. I told her sure, I would come. I knew that after yesterday's incident, I needed to get some direction. I needed God to help me. I knew the Lord had heard my prayers a few days ago and he was going to continue to make things better for me. I even invited Nathan to go to church and to my surprise, he wanted to go. The two of us got dressed and attended the service. It was very uplifting and the message that the Bishop preached was just for me. He brought the sermon from ***Matthew 12:25: "Every Kingdom divided against itself is brought to desolation; and every city or house divided against itself, shall not stand"***. I really thought about what he had read. I kept thinking to myself, a house divided. It was like God himself had showed me that when He says in His word that two should become one flesh that is just what it means. If the two are unequal, then they cannot survive as one. I said to God, "This is really deep!" The rest of the service was wonderful. A lot of people went up for altar call and I even went for prayer. I really hadn't made up my mind one hundred percent to come back to the Lord, but I knew it wouldn't be long now.

The following Monday, I went out to the county courthouse to a get a restraining order for Brian. I didn't want him anywhere near me or Little Brian. He had turned into a crazy man. I could see that the devil had really tricked me. What I needed to do was to continue to seek the Lord and I did exactly that. The next Sunday, when I went to Bishop Jenkins' church, an evangelist named Evangelist Jamie McClure was the speaker. I will never forget that day. She preached like I had never heard a woman preach. Everything she said cut like a knife. The tears began to flow as she began telling how women as a whole were in trouble. She had first hand experience being a wife of an abusive spouse, but in her case, it was physical. I personally knew what it was like to be emotionally and verbally abused.

Gwendolyn Jackson

She also said that if you have Jesus, that is all that you need. She told us that Jesus is able to heal you of a broken heart, a broken spirit and a broken life. Evangelist McClure said to the congregation, "Whatever your situation is today, come, Jesus wants to fix it for you, today." She told us not to be ashamed, the Lord loves you.

As I sat there with tears flowing, I began talking to the Lord. I said, "Lord, today is the day that I am coming back to you. You are married to a backslider and I am reuniting with you right now." I immediately jumped up and rushed to the altar. I began crying out to the Lord. The power of God was all over me. I began repenting with my whole heart. I felt a release deep within me. The burdens had been lifted, the sins had been forgiven, and the Lord had freed me that very moment from the chains of sin and had forgiven me for my disobedience to Him. All of a sudden, as I was worshipping and praising God, I began to speak in tongues. I had not done that in years. It was wonderful. This went on for more than an hour and a half. By the time I had settled back down, I knew something had happened to me that would change me for the rest of my life.

I was so excited when I got home, that I went to the basement to tell Nathan what had happened. He seemed very interested and I told him that the Lord had really moved in my life today and things were going to be all right. Nathan told me that he should have gone with me. He said he was tired of living the way he was and that he really wanted the Lord to come into his life. I invited him to come to service with me on Wednesday night.

I was walking on cloud twenty-nine and I knew that no devil in hell could steal my joy. Brian called. I decided quickly that I was going to be as civilized as possible and not let him steal my joy. He was saying some real crazy things to me, telling me how he had another woman, she had it going on and that she was going to take care of him like a real woman should. Brian went on to say that he was going to take Little Brian away from me and that's when I hit the roof. I asked him if he had lost the little

Thy Maker Is Thy Husband

piece of mind that he had left. I told him that hell would freeze over twice before he got Little Brian from me. I also told him that if he was going to call me with this kind of nonsense, not to call my house and I hung up the phone. I just sat on the bed, thinking of how sinister he had become. I began to wish that he would drop off the face of the earth.

Since Brian and I had separated, I had begun to have difficulty paying the rent and all of the other bills he had left behind. I felt it was probably best at that point to ask my parents if Brian Jr. and I could move back home for awhile. I really wanted to make it on my own and let Nathan live as a boarder, but he had lost his job and I didn't know how I would manage to get Brian to give me anything, so I definitely couldn't depend on him. My father gave me a long speech telling me that I had no business marrying that nappy headed boy anyway and for me to get myself back home and sit down for a while. I should have expected a speech because whenever one of us messed up, my father definitely let us know it, then he would usually come to our rescue. Within a couple of weeks, I had packed up everything and was back home. I had to first concentrate on getting my health back. I felt like I had been to hell and back. I told my mother I was quitting smoking as of that day, June 1, 1986. I went and got the rest of the cigarettes out of my purse and threw them in the trash. I had lost so much weight over the past few months; my mother was going to work on fattening me up. That terrible rash went away all by itself. I know it was stress related. I had read somewhere that stress does all kinds of stuff to a person's body and can kill you. I was a living witness!

Life for me was better now than it had been in a very long time. I had been growing closer to the Lord each day. It was so funny, that when I picked up my Bible a few days later to read, I was lost. I used to know the books of the Bible backwards and forward. Everything looked so strange to me, as if I was reading something I had never seen before. I just said to myself that the Lord would help me to remember again. I had to start somewhere.

Gwendolyn Jackson

Nathan called me and wanted to go to church with me on Sunday. He had already made up his mind that he wanted to give his life to Jesus Christ. The service was powerful. When the altar call was made, Nathan went up without hesitation. I just began to rejoice and praise God. I never would have thought that he would become a born again Christian. A few days later, Nathan was filled with the Holy Ghost. I tell you, God had really been moving. The Lord made Nathan into a brand new person overnight. We hung out, fellowshipped and worshipped God together. I called my friend Cynthia, whom I hadn't spoken with in a while. She told me that she could tell that something about me had changed because I seemed so calm. She wanted to know what was going on. I told her that I was back at Bishop Jenkins' church and was living a saved life once again and that it was great. Cynthia went on to tell me how her brother Tommy had become a born again Christian. I couldn't believe it. I said to her, "You mean the weed smoking king?"

She laughed and said yes. She said that she knew her brother was sincere because he did everything with his whole heart whether it was good or bad. She said Tommy was flirting with a lady who also happened to be a born again Christian and she had lead him to Jesus Christ. I thought to myself, Lord this is great. It seemed like the people you would have expected to be the least likely to become born again were changing their lives. I was floating on cloud nine.

I really liked my new job. A few months ago, I had started working at an HMO. Those were the new insurance programs for the future. It had been pretty nice so far. The thing was, we worked right inside the shopping center. I walked into work on this particular day just as I normally did and saw a piece of mail on my desk. Some woman that Brian had been living with happened to get some mail that belonged to me. She had opened it and wrote some nasty words all over it and mailed it to my job. Keep in mind, I hadn't been back in church very long, so I lost it. I got her phone number from my friend who worked at the phone company and called. I told her if she ever sent anything else to

Thy Maker Is Thy Husband

my job or called my house again, I would hurt her. She went on to tell me that Brian was a dog, who had taken all of her money and some of her jewelry and how she threw all his things out on the parking lot. She went on to tell me that she didn't want our mail coming to her house. She was using all kinds of foul language that wasn't even in my vocabulary. I told her that that is what happens when you mess with another person's husband. I had to pray and ask the Lord for help. I prayed hard that I wouldn't have to deal with Brian and any of his foolishness again. I was starting to feel that it might be a while before that prayer was answered.

Later that day, I got a phone call at work from one of Brian's associates. He told me that Brian said that I had called the police and snitched on him. That I had informed the police that he was dealing drugs.

First of all, I didn't know what this man did besides work at the airline where Brian used to work. Secondly, if I did know he was a drug dealer, I'm not sure that I would be running to tell police and put my life in danger. I told the associate that Brian was telling a damn lie. He told me O.K., so I guess he believed me. I was really upset. I guess Brian was trying to get me killed. I called him and told him that he was the scum of the earth. I told him something was going to happen to him if he kept going around giving people my number at work and telling lies that could put Little Brian and me in danger. I told him I was really sorry that he had fooled me in the way that he had, but if he was trying to set me up, he was messing with the wrong person. I told Brian that I was born again and anything that he did to try to harm me, God would see it. The Bible says that ***"No weapon formed against me shall prosper and every tongue that rises against me in judgment shall be condemned" Isaiah 54:17.*** Brian told me not to start that preaching crap with him, that he did tell his friend lies because he wanted to get back at me for calling the police on him and making him move out of the house. I told Brian that that was a bunch of garbage. He had forced my hand.

Gwendolyn Jackson

Brian didn't understand that he couldn't live the way he wanted and treat me like dirt and expect me to be there to put up with all the things he was doing to his son and me. I told him that he must be a crazy man. I told him that I was going to go and speak with a lawyer to file for divorce. I was not going to have anything else to do with him. I went on to tell Brian that he had succeeded in destroying our family and that I was going to give him just what he wanted. He refused to go to marriage counseling with Bishop Jenkins. He just didn't care. I had spoken with him about how I had refused Bishop Jenkins' counsel a few years ago when I had asked him to marry us. Now I was back in his office needing spiritual counseling to get out of the mess that the Lord had told me not to get into in the first place.

Bishop Jenkins read me a verse from ***Proverbs 19:21*** that said, ***"There are many devices in a man's heart; nevertheless, the counsel of the Lord that shall stand."*** I had never read that before and it was powerful. I told him how upset I was when he said he couldn't marry Brian and me. Bishop Jenkins didn't find that part to be very humorous. After speaking with him for more than an hour and a half, I told him that I wanted a divorce, that I couldn't stand it any longer. Bishop Jenkins told me that Brian's outwardly admitting to committing adultery was biblical grounds for a divorce. I was relieved to hear that. The word of God had allowed me to proceed with a divorce. He prayed for Brian and me. I felt very strange after leaving. I wasn't sure if I was happy or sad. I never would have thought Brian would turn on me the way he did. I was learning that only what you do for Christ lasts. We had made so many plans and now they had vanished.

As I drove home, warm, slow tears began rolling down my face. I began to think of the day that I had found out that Brian was living with a woman from his job. I had driven to her house early one Saturday morning and I couldn't believe that his car was parked outside. I didn't know what to do. I felt like breaking all her windows, but I knew that would only make matters worse. I wrote him a note and put it on his windshield so that he would know that I had found where he had been every night. Later on, he told me that they were both afraid when they came out and found the note. It was hurtful to know that the person you thought you would be with for the rest of your life would crush and break your heart the way Brian did mine. I stopped thinking about that and started singing a song by this new gospel singing group, Commissioned. I remember that some of the words in the song went something like this: "Cry on, God understands your tears, He knows how much you can bear, in this trial here. Cry on, when there's nothing else to say and he'll wipe all your tears away." The song ended with "Weeping may endure for the night, but joy comes in the morning time." That song touched me very deeply.

As the months passed, the Lord began to wipe away my tears. I was excited about the Lord: on a mission winning souls. In the next six months, I believed I had led seven young men to the Lord. It had been exciting. My good friend Cynthia and her boyfriend Tony both were baptized at my church and Cynthia received the gift of the Holy Ghost. God had been moving by His spirit and I had been concentrating on helping God build His Kingdom and I knew He was going to help me.

Eight months had passed since Brian and I had separated. I had been putting off filing for divorce, but I knew that I had to do it very soon. I received a pay increase on my job and I decided to move out of my parents' home and get Brian Jr. and me our own place. I had found a very nice two bedroom duplex in the suburbs in a very quiet neighborhood. As a matter of fact, the duplex was brand new and the people who owned it were Christians. My credit was not great, but they went ahead and gave me a chance, allowing me to move in after I had explained my situation. I knew that was really a blessing. It was nice to be in my own place again, but it was also pretty lonely at times. I became good friends with Cynthia's brother, Tommy. That brother was really on fire for the Lord and I really enjoyed our friendship. He moved to California and wanted Brian Jr. and me to come visit. I told him I would when summer came.

During the next couple of months, Brian and I became civil with one another again. For Brian Jr's sake, we even went out to eat a couple of times. One night, I was lying in bed when Brian called to apologize. He told me that he had really been thinking about all the things that he had done to Brian Jr. and me and that he really missed us and wanted to know if I would think about giving our marriage another chance. He asked me if I would forgive him for all the things that he had done and said. Brian also told me that he didn't mess around with cocaine any longer. I listened to everything he said and I really wanted to believe him and say yes, come home right now, but I couldn't. I told him to let me think about it for awhile and maybe he could come by on the weekend and we could talk. He told me that he loved me and hoped I would make the right decision. I hung up the phone, fell to the floor and said, "Oh Lord, why now?" I had just begun to get adjusted to being a single parent and accepting the fact that Brian and I were going to be divorced and now this! I feared living life as a single woman, but at the same time, I couldn't even begin to forget all the things Brian had put me through the last couple of years.

Then I started thinking about the scripture in *1 Corinthians 7:13* that says: *"And the woman which hath an husband that believeth not, and if he be pleased to dwell with her, let her not leave him."* I knew from my counseling sessions with Bishop Jenkins that I still had a right to divorce Brian, but I just didn't know what to do.

Brian came by and we sat in the living room and talked for a very long time. I explained to him that I was not the same person any more. I had given my whole life to the Lord and I was never going to start living the way I had again. I told Brian that I didn't drink any kind of alcohol, nor did I listen to any kind of secular music. I had really become a new person. Brian went on to say that he loved me just as I was and if I had made a change for the better, then he would too. I also asked him if he

Thy Maker Is Thy Husband

would start going to church with Brian Jr. and me and he said that he wanted his family back and would do whatever it took to make it work. I took that to be a yes. Brian left that night and went back to his apartment to get his things. He then came back and sat down and got all of our business papers together. He said that on pay day, he would bring his check home and let me take care of all the household finances and for me to give him just enough money for gas, haircuts and lunch.

Things were beautiful for a while. It seemed like we were going to make it. We decided that we were going to buy a new car. This was the second new car we had brought since we had married. It was a very nice Buick Regal. But a few days afterwards, Brian started acting a little strange. I pulled into the driveway after work one evening and he was smoking a joint as he was working on his car. I jumped out of the car and I said, "No way! This is Holy Ground; you can not smoke that mess here! I knew it was too good to be true." I hadn't seen him smoking weed or anything for three months, but I guess he couldn't keep faking me out. I went into the house to the master bathroom where I normally pray and began to cry out to the Lord. Brian heard me, came to the door and said, "What is wrong with you?" I was praying in the spirit and I guess he thought I was going crazy. I didn't answer him right away. I came out a few minutes later and said, "Brian, there is nothing wrong with me. I was praying in the spirit and I am not going to let Satan take over anymore in my life."

"I'll be back later," he said. When he got back at 2:00 a.m., I asked him where he had been. He said he had been hanging out with Dre, one of his childhood friends.

Things began to deteriorate. One Saturday night, Brian went out to the club and didn't get in until six the following morning. I told him that we had to talk, that he was not going to start that mess with me again and the devil was a lie if he thought I would go through all that hell again. All of a sudden, Brian turned to me and cursed the name of the Lord. He used that ugly four-letter word and told me to _____ the Holy Ghost. I was petrified for him. I told Brian he had just sowed some terrible seeds and he had better pray to the Lord to forgive him. He didn't seem to care. I told him that some day he was going to reap what he sowed and that I hoped he was able to take it. Brian told me he decided that he really did not want to be married anymore. This life just wasn't for him. He wanted to go ahead with the divorce.

I guess I had doubted that our marriage would really work out. I was hurt once again, but this time, the pain was not so severe. Then I became angry. I told Brian that by the time I got home from work, I wanted him to be out of my house. For the past month he hadn't paid any of the bills. I told him that before I let a man lay up on me for free, I would go to a homeless shelter! I also told him, if everything that belonged to him was not out of there, that he could find it in the middle of the street. I was really wrong for saying that, but I was angry. I really felt bad for Brian Jr. because he was old enough to realize that his daddy had been here with us and now he was gone. Brian had convinced me to trade our first car in, that was paid for and I could not afford to keep the new one, so I was now left with this old car that Brian had bought. He told me I could drive it. I told him that my Father in heaven is rich and I didn't have to drive that old car.

Within a few days, Kayla came by. I hadn't seen her for quite sometime. She had lost a lot of weight, colored her hair and had quite a bit of gold jewelry on. When we got in her car, she had Kenny G tapes and everything. I couldn't believe it! I asked her what was going on. Kayla had always been an inspiration, was always concerned about my soul and even loved me when I was backsliding. I was really concerned about her. She told me that she was having a little fun. I informed her to be careful and not to let the devil trick her like he had me. She said that she wouldn't take it that far, but I told her I didn't mean too either and look at what had happened to me. She just got quiet on me. I changed the topic and began to tell her about my dilemma with the car and with Brian.

Thy Maker Is Thy Husband

Kayla took me to a car dealership where this guy she had once dated worked. Her friend's name was Greg. He was a very nice Christian person. He was very helpful and took us on test drives in a lot of cars. I explained my situation to him and told him that I didn't have any money. I mean zilch, nada, nothing! He said he would see what he could do. I started praying and I knew that the Lord was going to make a way out of no way for me. By the time the day was over, I had a brand new Mazda 626 LX, not a just a 626, but the top of the line. I just thanked and praised God for the Blessing!

A few days later, Brian stopped by with one of his friends to get the rest of his belongings. He saw the car in the driveway and the first thing he said was; "Whose car is that?" I said to him, "Didn't I tell you that my Father is rich?" I told him it was mine, that God had blessed me with it when I didn't have any money. I didn't feel it was any of his business. He had done what he wanted to do. He wanted to be single and enjoy life. Whatever was going on in my life from then on was my business.

The weeks and summer months were passing on. I had promised Cynthia's brother, Tommy that I would come and visit him in California. So Brian Jr. and I went to San Diego for a week. We had a blast. Tommy and a friend shared a one-bedroom apartment and they let me have the room for the week. It was crowded, but we had a great time. I think I slept for a total of sixteen hours out of the whole week. The church that he attended was on fire! They had praise dancers that opened the worship services and their pastor was anointed. It was a blessed time. Tommy could throw down in the kitchen. I was surprise that a guy could cook so well. That was the best vacation I had ever taken. It was time to return to the real world. I think Tommy was a little sad to see us leave. I remember when he used to smoke weed with Brian now three years later, we were praising the Lord together.

During that summer, I felt that the Lord wanted me to change churches. I began attending True Vine Christian

Gwendolyn Jackson

Fellowship. The pastors were Lewis and Debbie Richards. I was excited about the change. The Lord was using me at Bishop Jenkins' church, but I felt that the Lord wanted me to move on. The Richards were what they called – Faith Teachers and I needed a lot of that during that time. The pastors were very understanding about my situation and I will never forget what Pastor Lewis told me one morning when I was dropping Brian Jr. off at the church daycare center. He told me that the Lord was going to bless me exceedingly and abundantly above anything I could ask for or think of. I said to myself, that that was pretty deep. I guess I really didn't comprehend what he was saying, but it sounded good and I figured one day, I would understand. The Lord continued to use me in leading men and women to Christ at my new church.

A short while before the Thanksgiving Holiday, I was doing my dual parents' duties with Brian Jr. and we had to make a trip to the barbershop. As I was waiting for Brian Jr., a young man began talking to me, wanting to know my name etc,. etc. I couldn't wait to get the chance and jump in and start witnessing to him about Jesus Christ. To my surprise, he was receptive to what I was saying to him. We finally decided to exchange names. His name was Brandon Cook. It had been a long time since I had an up and close personal conversation with a male. It felt sort of awkward. The only thing I knew to talk about was Jesus. The barbershop was up the street from our family store and Brandon asked me if he could walk me back down to the store. As we were walking, Brandon began to ask me question about my church. He told me that he hadn't received Jesus Christ as his personal savior before. He went to church when he was a child, but that was about it. This young man then asked me for my phone number and told me that he would like to go to church with me on Sunday if I didn't mind picking him up. I don't know what's wrong with so many men, none of them had wheels. I didn't understand. I started talking to the Lord, asking him if I should go pick up this strange man and take him to

Thy Maker Is Thy Husband

church. I told Brandon to give me a call and I would let him know later that night.

I picked Brandon up for church and he received the Lord Jesus and became a born again Christian. The Lord is awesome. He caused me to go to the barbershop on this particular Saturday because of His omniscient powers. He knew Brandon would be there for me to witness to. God is so amazing. Brandon and I began to spend a lot of time together. He really was crazy about Brian Jr. and me. He was moving pretty fast with me. I remember one day, he caught the bus to my job and bought me a gift from one of the stores in the mall. He was a very sensitive man. He acted very mature for his age. He was only twenty-six and acted every bit of thirty-six. Brandon had gone through a lot of changes in his life and I guess just like me, hard times made you grow up fast.

The Christmas holidays were quickly approaching once again. This year was sort of special, having someone in my life to spend it with. I kept telling myself to take it slow and not to move too fast. I had to keep in mind that he was a new babe in Christ and I didn't want to hinder his Christian growth. Brandon wanted to kiss me and hug quite a bit. I knew that we had to be careful with that, because the word tells us not to give place to the devil. Those emotions and feelings start to rise up quickly and if you don't watch out, you will find yourself in trouble. Brandon would always tell me that he was falling in love with me, but I didn't want to deal with it. Brian and I were still going through with the divorce and I wanted to get that behind me first.

I couldn't believe what Brian did on Christmas Eve. Brandon and I went on a date and when we got back, Brian was at my parents' house bringing Brian Jr. his Christmas gift. He tried to be very cordial and sensible with Brandon, introducing himself and all that. Then he told me that he wanted to see me in private. Brian wanted to know who this dude was I was dating. I told him that it wasn't any of his business. Brian insisted that it was, telling me that I was still his wife and always would be no matter what I did in this lifetime. I told him that he couldn't

Gwendolyn Jackson

make me feel guilty. I had sought the Lord and was freed from this marriage. Free to go on with my life, that he should do the same. Brian continued for a few minutes, saying how much he missed me and how I was mistreating him. As I was showing Brian to the door, he turned to me and told me that I would be getting an invitation in mail soon. He went on to say that he was getting married in July, to someone by the name of Sandra. He would like me to be there. To top that off, she was sitting in car waiting for him the entire time he was putting on this fake performance in the house with me. I just laughed at Brian and told him that he was really a sad person. I really felt sorry for him and I told him to have a nice life with Sandra.

Brian had really stooped low. We weren't even divorced, yet he had the nerve to get engaged to someone else. I knew that I had really done the right thing by getting out of the marriage. A few days afterwards, Brian told me that some other woman had called to say that she was pregnant by him. I told him that he was a joke, engaged, fathering children and he was technically still a married man. As I told him once before, you are definitely going to reap what you have sown. I was really hurt by all of the things that Brian had done, but I was determined not to let them get to me. The next time Brandon and I got together, I felt a little differently about him. I felt that maybe, I should allow him to get a little bit closer to me and let him be there for me through the divorce. I just didn't want to risk the chance of falling into sin.

The New Year's Eve Service was great. Brandon and I went out to dinner before going to church and we had a very nice evening. It was a very cold winter night and I had begun to fall for Brandon. I thought it was so nice having a young man in my life who was a born again and a spirit-filled believer. Brandon told me that he really loved me and he felt that the Lord had told him that I was going to be his wife. I didn't know how to take that, but I knew that night that we didn't want to be apart. The next thing I knew, Brandon and I were at a hotel, way out in the country. I had called home and told my mother that I would be

Thy Maker Is Thy Husband

back by the break of day. Brandon and I became very passionate that night and before we both knew it, we had given in to our emotions and fallen into sin. I was afraid of this happening, but it seemed as if both of us needed someone to hold on to and to feel loved.

The next day, I really felt embarrassed coming home at ten in the morning. I didn't explain. I told them that Brandon and I had a long date. I kept saying to myself, I know my family is thinking that I am proclaiming to be saved and spirit-filled, but I had stayed out all night with a man. I went straight to my room and started praying and asking for God's forgiveness. Brandon came by later that day. We talked about what had happened the previous night. He thought it was beautiful. I explained to him that we couldn't allow that to happen if we were not married and were professing to be born again and spirit-filled Christians. He didn't understand how it could be so wrong, especially when he felt that I was going to be his wife. We continued to fall into sin on a regular basis and turned around and went to church two and three times a week. After Brandon had been attending church with me for a while and began to receive and understand some of the teachings, he got up in church one Sunday morning and said that the Lord had given him a word for the church. I couldn't believe he had done that. I wasn't sure that he even understood what prophecy was and how it operated in the church. I didn't say anything. The Lord had begun to deal with me about Brandon. I knew that if he was going to be all that God wanted him to be, that our relationship would be a hindrance to him at this time. I could not deny the fact that I knew the word. But the Lord had brought to my remembrance a scripture in **Hebrew 12:1: "Wherefore seeing we also are compassed about with so great a cloud of witnesses, let us lay aside every weight and sin which doth so easily beset us and let us run with patience the *race that is set before us."*** I realized that I was a weight on Brandon and he was one on me.

My court date had finally come- the day of reckoning. The life that I had known for the past six and a half years was about to end. It was still hard for me to believe that sometimes this man I had loved so dearly and thought that I would spend my entire life with would cause me so much pain and wound me so deeply. I had to face the facts and I knew that the Lord's word is true and stands forever. The Lord let me know that only what you do for Him will last. My house was built on sinking sand and it did not stand. It was a house divided.

When I arrived at the courthouse, Brian wasn't there. I was sort of relieved. I would have had to deal with him. Towards the very end of the court session, Brian walked through the door and sat at the very back of the courtroom. By that time the divorce proceedings had ended. The judge saw Brian come in and asked him if he had anything he would like to say. Brian told him no. We ended up on the same elevator and there was complete silence. As Brian got off, he turned around, looked at me and walked off.

Meanwhile, Brandon was back at my house babysitting Brian Jr. When I got home, I had to dry my tears before going in. I didn't want him to see me so vulnerable. As soon as I came in, Brandon came up to me and hugged me very tight. He said that I belonged to him now and he would like to be engaged by June. I immediately told him that there wasn't any chance of me marrying anyone anytime soon. I needed to get myself together and find out who I really was. Brandon didn't take that well. He gave me an ultimatum. He told me that we either get married in the next few months, or he didn't want to continue the relationship. At that point in my life, I didn't want to deal with anymore confusion, nor was I able to even comprehend the thought of being married again. Brandon couldn't understand that I needed time to heal from the past marriage and that I needed to grieve, go through my problems and lean on the Lord. I felt that it would be best for both of us if we went our separate ways.

After a few days, late one night, Brandon called crying and sobbing. I wasn't in the mood to deal with any man or his problems. Brandon had come along at a very difficult time in my life. It seemed as if he was trying to force me to fall in love with him and marry him on a whim. I couldn't seem to get it through his thick head that I was not mentally or emotionally prepared to deal with a marriage again. For several weeks this went on. Brandon would call my mother, begging her to talk to me. What Brandon didn't realize was that he wouldn't be able to force this relationship on me. As time went on, the pressure from Brandon eased. He began to realize that he had a lot of things in life to heal from as I did. Two wounded souls trying to make it together, feeling sorry for each other, would not be a strong relationship. As I was reading the Word, I came across a scripture that really spoke straight to me. It read: *"Except the Lord build the house, they labor in vain that build it" Psalms 127:1.*

CHAPTER 6

SINGLE AND SEARCHING

After my divorce, it took me some time to get used to the single life again. Things had changed a lot. I hadn't realized how much you had to go through to get back into that lifestyle. The difference for me was that now I was also a single parent. I saw so many books and magazines in the store about single parenting. Society made it appear as though it was a cool thing. It was definitely not so. Many people do a great job of being a single parent and I believed that I would be one of those people. But deep inside I dreaded the thought of my son growing up without a father in the home. One of the first things I decided to do for myself was to get a makeover. My girlfriend Cynthia had asked me for years to get some contact lenses and I thought, "Now is the time." While I was turning over a new leaf, I decided to go for the gusto. I colored my hair, got a short haircut and did myself over.

One afternoon, I went out to the mall just to see if I still had it. I knew that wasn't what Christian women did! Right…Those brothers at church acted so stuffy; like they thought someone was hunting them down like wild deer. So I never even gave any of them the impression I was interested in them. As I strolled down the mall, I got a couple of winks and I was confident that I still had it!

Summer 1988 had rolled in and my catering business was doing really well. I had never known I had it in me to do this kind of work. Cooking and preparing food was therapy for me. I enjoyed seeing people eating and enjoying my cooking. The Lord was really blessing Brian Jr. and me. Things were working out so differently than I had thought. I thought I would be sad and depressed after divorce, but the Lord was comforting me daily and he always reminded me that the *"Joy of the Lord is my strength." (Nehemiah 8:10).*

Thy Maker Is Thy Husband

Brian called to ask if I would let Brian Jr. be a part of his wedding. I started to give him a hard time, but I decided that I was not going to give the devil any room to attack me. I guessed this was Brian's way of throwing his new wife in my face. But it didn't work. I went right along with the program. I dropped Brian Jr. off at his grandmother's for the wedding and Brian came in, looking like seven miles of bad highway, not at all like someone who was getting married that afternoon. I didn't have much to say to him. I just told him to be sure Brian Jr. got home at a decent hour and to have a nice wedding and a wonderful life. I do admit though, there was a tad bit of sarcasm in my remark, but I couldn't help myself.

Seven months had passed since my last date. Most of my time was spent with my son, serving the Lord and attending to my part-time catering business. Chris, my high school sweetheart, called me one day. He was in the Navy and stationed in Norfolk, Virginia. I was glad to hear from him. He called to tell me that he had gotten involved in some illegal activity while he was stationed in Southern California. He had been court-martialed and faced possible time in prison. But thanks be to God, the Lord sent him back to St. Louis shortly afterwards. While in St. Louis, we went to church and out to dinner. We had a wonderful time reminiscing. All of a sudden, Chris got serious. It seemed pretty strange coming from him, he was always the comedian. I let him know right away that I could only be his friend, as I had been for the past eight years and that I couldn't get serious with him. Deep inside, I had a fear of the Lord and I didn't want to experience any more failed relationships that were formed outside of God's perfect will for my life. Chris thought I had turned into a religious fanatic. That was not the case at all. I had realized that there was a terrible price to pay when you got involved in things outside of God's will when you belong to him. You must and will pay a dear price. My soul and spirit could not afford to risk that again.

Before I knew it, I had fallen into the trap that the devil had set for me. Knowingly, I continued seeing Chris; playing with fire and I got burned. Falling in love again. I wanted to slap myself. I couldn't believe I had done it again. There were no excuses for me. The word had been sown in my heart on good ground and watered on a daily basis, but some how, some way, I had fallen right back into that same old sinful trap.

One day I asked myself, "Why is it that I can't seem to stand firm when it comes to being tempted in the area of sexual relations?" I really didn't have an answer, but there was an open door in my life that I thought had been closed. There was still a crack in the door for the enemy to get in. Chris and I carried on this empty and false relationship. Chris didn't have a car and he was not aggressively looking for a job. One day, on my lunch hour, I went to the police department in one of the county municipalities to get a job application. Chris filled it out and I turned it in for him. A few days later, Chris was called for an interview and testing for a position. He didn't even go. I had had enough of these sorry, non-aggressive, broke men. Relationships are such a joke. I told myself that the next man that I have a relationship with, God would have to drop out of the sky. "Something is wrong with these brothers", I thought. "I can't understand how a grown man doesn't have enough 'get up and go' to make sure he has his own wheels, even if it is a hoopty. No jobs – nothing!" One couldn't help but wonder if we women were at fault for allowing them to lay up on us and take care of them. Somehow our roles had gotten mixed up. Sister girl was not going for it. I was a child of the King and knew I deserved God's best. Thank God I hadn't gotten thrown off my path completely. I thank the Lord for His goodness and His mercies that were and are brand new every morning.

The windows of heaven were opening up for me. I received a promotion on my job to a department that would allow me to make more money than I had ever dreamed of. For such a long time, I had been a tither and a giver, but it seemed as though I was barely able to pay my car payment and rent at times. I had to constantly listen to tapes from Pastor Lewis teachings on faith and trusting the Lord. Each morning, I would read the scripture

Thy Maker Is Thy Husband

from *Malachi 3:10* in which God makes certain promises to the tither. I had to remember that God is not a man, that he should lie; neither the son of man, that he should repent; hath he spoken and shall he not make it good? For me, trusting God's word had paid off. Without a husband in the home, God was showing me that He was more than able to take care of me. I sought the Lord for understanding and tried to hear what he was telling me. In my heart, I felt that he was telling me that He was all that I needed and that I would be fine. But I wasn't sure. Maybe when I get a chance, I thought, it would be good to share this with Pastor Lewis.

Things were really busy at work in my new department. Each work day would be over before I knew it. The two young ladies I worked with were a lot of fun and we got along well from the start. One day, after work, I knew I looked like fifteen miles of bad highway, but I didn't care. Before the end of the day, I would normally go into the restroom and fix my hair and makeup before driving home. But this day, I just didn't care. As I was driving past the university, a young man passed me in the sharp black BMW convertible. He even tried to flirt. I just played it down and said, "No thanks." As I proceeded to drive on my normal route home, the lane I was traveling in was at a dead stop. I sat for five minutes trying to get over and when I looked over my shoulder to change lanes, the guy in the BMW let me over. As he kept driving right along with me, he rolled down his window and tried to introduce himself to me. Of all days, when I looked like a worn out dish rag, someone like this was flirting with me. Stranger things had happened, I guessed. When we reached the traffic signal, he asked me to pull on to the restaurant parking lot. I said to myself, "I will use this as an opportunity to witness." This smooth looking fellow got out of his sharp car and walked over to my car. Mind you, I was ready to speed off, just in case he tried something crazy. As he was standing there talking to me, I was thinking to myself, "Maybe there are some men out here that want something in life?" He seemed excited that I was even talking to him. We parked and chatted for a few minutes. He was quick to let me know he had a job; telling me that he was on his way to work. We exchanged phone numbers and then went our separate ways. Ten minutes later, I stopped at the grocery store and almost the exact same thing happened. I met another clean-cut, decent looking fellow in the store. He walked me to my car and we exchanged phone numbers. Meanwhile, as we were standing there, someone let a grocery cart roll into his brand new Maxima and broke his tail light. Of course that was a major upset. He left and went back into the store and dealt with his problem.

In less than twenty-four hours, the young man I had met in traffic called. Seeming very polite, he introduced himself as Stephen Henderson, but told me to call him Steve. Steve told me his whole life story in fifteen minutes. He worked the second shift at McDonnell Douglas, had never married and had a four year old son. Steve told me that he and his mother had bought a home in the county and he was just a hard working young man trying to make it in the white man's world. He let me know up front that he was not a phony and that "what you see is what you get." Steve asked if I would like to go out with him on Saturday, so we could get to know each other a little more. My response was yes. Steve was a year and a half younger than me, but seemed pretty mature and up on things in the world and around him.

Saturday evening felt like I was sixteen all over again. It had been almost two years since I had been out on a real date. Butterflies were buzzing in my stomach. Steve arrived around eight to pick me up. I went from every guy that I had met lately not having a car at all, to a guy that had one of the best cars on the road. I hadn't realized how much attention you got riding down the street in a luxury car with a nice looking couple as its' occupants. I could see how people could get use to the attention. It felt pretty nice. We both decided that we wanted our first date to be simple, so we went to a little Italian eatery in the preppy part of town; where people of Steve's caliber hung out. Our conversation was very open and honest. I let him know up front

Thy Maker Is Thy Husband

that I was a born again Christian; trying to do the right thing and raise my son. That seemed to impress him very much. I told him about my divorce and I was honest and told him I was still healing from that ordeal. Steve told me about his son, their relationship and the relationship that never was with his son's mother. He also told me some of his dreams and aspirations. I had never met such a young man with confidence. He appeared to be the type of man that wanted to take charge and needed a woman that was able to keep up with his drive for success. "By any means necessary", was his motto. Steve had a driving force inside him that was almost spooky, but I was fascinated by his dreams and apparently he was making it happen or at least someone was. As the night went on, we talked and laughed and ate our food. It seemed as though we had known each other for years. We stayed until we were thrown out of the restaurant. It was freezing cold that night, so we sort of hugged while running to the car, trying to keep warm. Before Steve dropped me off, we drove through a very nice, upper scale neighborhood. Steve told me that maybe one day, he and I would share a lovely house together. This was all pretty deep. It was three a.m. when Steve dropped me off. It had been a nice, clean fun evening no temptation-nothing but nice clean fun. I laid in bed that night thinking of how refreshing that was for me. I wasn't sure of what to think. Lately the Lord had really been pouring out his blessings on me and I just wondered, "Is this part of the package?" For several months, I had been taking it slow and trying very hard to wait on the Lord for Mr. Right and I just wondered... I had struggled with being single and celibate. I knew the Lord said in his word, that He would not allow me to be tempted above that which I was able to bear, so He knew exactly what I needed and when I needed it.

Our company Christmas party was in a couple of days. I really wanted to go this year. I had never gone in the past because I never had a date. I got enough nerve to call Steve and ask him on a date. Not only did Steve accept my invitation but told me he would even take off work to be my date. He picked me up and asked if I would like to drive the BMW. I really wanted to, but I acted like it wasn't really a big deal and told him no thank you, I just wanted to be chauffeured tonight. He smiled and said O.K. All eyes were on us when we walked in the door. Steve said he was going to play his role with the white folks on tonight. Tonight I felt like Cinderella and the Prince had picked me up in his carriage. More and more, I was hoping this was it for me; my dreams come true in a relationship. I had to remember to be careful and stay prayerful, because I couldn't afford to be tricked again by the devil. After the party, we took the scenic route home. Steve was playing Kenny G in his car and the music was so relaxing; the night was just short of being perfect.

Steve took me to his home to meet his mother. Mothers made me nervous. I'm a mother too and I know how we are about our sons. We want the best for them. I had to make a good impression on her. No sooner had she heard his key in the door, she called him. I could hear her chewing him out about taking off work to go to the Christmas party with me. I might as well head up the road, because that did not impress her. I heard two sets of footsteps heading towards the living room. She introduced herself as Darlene Henderson and told me, "I don't mind you seeing my son, but he can't miss work for parties. I said yes ma'am. I could tell Steve was so embarrassed, but then she sort of laughed and we played it off. The old girl was dead serious. They had a beautiful home, which looked like something straight out of the House Beautiful magazine. All kinds of questions were running through my mind, nice looking; nice car; laid out house; not only a job, but a good job; not married; and no woman. Maybe he had someone else, but didn't tell me. I just couldn't quite figure it out but I knew time would tell.

Steve was a very spontaneous individual. One day, out of the blue, he called me at work and wanted me to make plans for us to take our two sons on vacation to Florida. No one could tell me he was not the one for me. It was the best vacation I had

Thy Maker Is Thy Husband

ever taken. Euphoria was an understatement to describe the time that we had. We were like the family that I had always dreamed of having. Our two sons got along. We were so much alike, that we almost had the exact same outfits packed for our boys. Steve wanted to know why I always talked about marriage. I had to explain to him, that I had problems being in serious relationships–especially when intimacy was involved and marriage was not the end result. Steve and I had begun to become intimate. At first, it was a few isolated times, then it became the norm.

One Sunday, I could have crawled under the seat during our morning worship. Pastor Lewis had always prophesied great things in my life. I had been told not only by Pastor Lewis, but by many others, that I had a great calling to God on my life and that God was going to use me to bring many souls into the Kingdom of God. Right now, I wasn't too sure about that. Pastor Lewis had a prayer line in front of the church for individuals who were seeking the Lord and to be filled with the Holy Spirit. All of a sudden, he called me to the front of the church to work the prayer line with him. I just about died. I kept saying to myself, "Lord, you know that I have been falling into sin; fornicating up a storm, even drinking amaretto sours every now and then. Why in the world is the Pastor calling me up there?" The Lord reminded me that His gifts and callings are without repentance. Maybe the Lord promised someone that they would be filled on that day and sure enough, when I prayed for them, they were filled. It wasn't that my faith in God had changed, but I felt convicted that I was praying for people to be filled with the Holy Spirit, while my life was not what it should have been at the time. I wondered why Pastor Lewis didn't discern in his spirit that something just wasn't right with me. Nevertheless, God had him call me up there for a reason.

After that situation happened, I sort of backed away from Steve for awhile. I told him that I needed to see where I needed to be at that point in my life. My friend Tommy was getting

Gwendolyn Jackson

married in San Diego and I told Steve that I would speak with him when I got back.

Life was really strange. I couldn't believe that Brian had the nerve to start calling me again. His new wife had left him and he had become addicted to crack cocaine. I felt so sorry for him and I really wanted to help him. Brian and his cousin Nathan were both good friends of Tommy, so we all decided to go out to San Diego for the wedding. Brian had lost everything-his car, his home, and his family. Nathan and I decided to put our money together and buy Brian's plane ticket, hoping that maybe a change of pace would help him get a better outlook on life. I could never tell Steve that I took Brian with me to San Diego. He had a very low opinion of anyone addicted to crack. Anyway, we took this ill-fated trip to the wedding. The ceremony was very nice. Tommy and his new wife had made very nice arrangements for all of us to stay at the hotel where they worked. Cynthia, her parents and fiancée all came out to the wedding as well. While in California, Brian and I visited one of my favorite places-La Jolla. I thought back to the days when Brian and I were first married and living in California and how we would go to the secluded areas on the beach and have our own private picnics. As he and I drove up to La Jolla, I kept wondering if some of those old feelings would come back. Unfortunately, the drive was not very enjoyable. I don't think Brian even knew how to relax and enjoy himself anymore. He wanted to disappear from all of us Jesus-talking folks and find himself some crack cocaine, I guess. It was a waste of time, money and effort bringing him out here. His very presence dampened my spirits.

Thank God! It was time to get back to St. Louis and to Steve. Brian had been out all night with the rental car and no one had seen any sign of him. I was getting very angry. We had to catch our flight in less than one hour and he had not returned with the car. Finally, at the last minute, he came walking into the hotel lobby, looking like something that the cat dragged in. I just looked at him and shook my head.

Thy Maker Is Thy Husband

The flight back to St. Louis was very eventful. Brian didn't feel very well and wanted to lay his head on my shoulder and sleep. After a while, he jumped up out of his seat and told me that his stomach was hurting and to get him something. I stood up to go into the overhead compartment, when he suddenly fell to the floor and went into a seizure. I freaked out!!! I began screaming for help. Thank God there was a doctor on board who revived him. The situation was so serious that we almost had to make an emergency landing. "Lord, why me?" I asked. I couldn't believe that we almost made national news. When the plane finally arrived in St. Louis, an ambulance was there to take him to the hospital. As usual, I ended up right in the middle of the mess. I got off the plane on the runway and into an ambulance with my ex-husband.

Later that day, I found out that Brian's episode was linked to crack cocaine consumption. I made up my mind that I was not going to get involved with him and his problems any longer. The hospital contacted Mrs. Williams and she took it from there. I tried to reach Brian's wife to let her know what happened to him, but found out that she had divorced him earlier in the year. He didn't even know that he was divorced. Now, that was pretty pathetic! I had to put Brian in the hands of the Lord.

That evening when I saw Steve, he made me forget everything that had happened the last couple of days. I just let him believe that I went to the wedding with my friends. Our relationship was beginning to take form now. Ms. Henderson and I had become very good friends. My catering business was doing quite well and Ms. Henderson and I began to work together. We worked like clock work and everything flowed like a calm stream Steve and I began to have talks about our future plans. My thoughts and plans seemed to be for the near and immediate future, while Steve had thoughts and plans for a possible future with me, but he didn't seem to be interested in doing anything any time soon. That often troubled me. Deep inside I had to face the fact that I was missing the mark and falling short of the Glory of God in my life. I had fallen in love with this man who made me feel like a whole woman. Steve had a way of building my self-esteem and confidence. I felt as though I could conquer anything that was placed before me. Steve was on the go all the time. Sometimes I wouldn't hear from him or see him for days at a time. That really got on my nerves, but he was always worth the wait. My friends weren't thrilled with the fact that I was dating Steve. Kayla had the nerve to tell me that. Apparently she had a problem with it, but I didn't care what she thought. One day she asked me what Steve's license plate number was, because she thought she had seen him on the freeway. That really ticked me off. She hadn't met him before, but I guess she was tripping off the fact that I told her that he had a convertible BMW and she wanted to see if I was telling the truth. Though I could see how someone may think I was fabricating this story because Steve was never around to meet any of my friends and was always on the move.

My dream for this season of miracles was for Steve to ask me to marry him. His son practically lived at my house on the weekends. We spent a lot of time together. Steve often said I would make someone a good wife, but he never would make a direct statement concerning us. Well, the holidays had come and gone and NO, I didn't receive a ring or anything close to it. Steve gave me a piece of black art work. He thought the woman on the picture reminded him of me. That was nice and all, but I was ready for some sort of commitment. On Valentine's Day, two dozen carnations and two dozen balloons were delivered to me with one giant heart-shaped balloon from Steve. I mean he went out big. I kept saying to myself that maybe, after two dozen carnations and balloons, tonight would be the night he proposed. The love of my life even took off work early to make our evening special.

While I was preparing our Valentine's Day dinner, the telephone rang. It was Chris! He wanted to know if I would marry him. I burst out laughing and told him no! Chris told me that he was serious. Well I had to be a heart breaker and let Chris know that I had a new love and things were pretty serious,

Thy Maker Is Thy Husband

at least from my point of view. Chris just told me goodbye and discontinued the conversation. Personally, I thought it was a joke that he would have the nerve to even ask me such a ridiculous question. It is so funny because the person that you would give anything to marry didn't seem to ask the question. Our evening was perfect, but the words "will you marry me?" never came up. As a matter of fact, Steve told me that sometimes he felt that I was too good for him. This man told me that he was too messed up to marry anyone. From the outside it seemed like he had it all together, but only he knew what was really going on inside his head.

Steve's birthday was coming up. A weekend away together would be the perfect opportunity to be alone and maybe he would see how good we were together. I had made reservations at a lakefront condo. I was very excited. I called Steve and told him to pack just his bags and bring his golf clubs; his woman was taking him away. Steve was one who showed little emotion, but I could tell that this really touched him. The day before Steve and I were supposed to leave on our trip, he called me with some lame story about him having to go out of town to some amateur boxing contest. I knew that he once boxed, but I hadn't seen one boxing match here in town. I couldn't help it. Steve got a piece of my mind and then some. He wanted me to call and change the reservations for another weekend that was more accommodating to his schedule. I told him that he made me sick. We were always doing everything that Steve wanted to do, when he wanted to do it. And I was just about sick of it. I told Steve just to forget it, we weren't going anywhere-period. He told me I was blowing things out of proportion. I was pretty upset about the whole thing. I had just had enough of men running my life and I wasn't going to let him do it to me; especially when I was trying to do something nice.

Days passed and not a word from Steve. When I finally get a decent man, something stupid like this had to happen. Quality time was very important in relationships. Time was one thing Steve did not have enough of. Not only for me, but for his son as well. Instead of us doing things together with the boys on the weekends, he would always bring his son and plenty of money for the three of us to have nice weekends. I normally did not see him again until the following Sunday. I loved him just that much to settle for it, but not anymore. I finally knew who I was and no matter how much money and status a man had, it was not enough for me to spend countless hours alone. I figured I would see him soon.

Sunday nights were pretty lonely now that Steve and I had broken off our relationship. I got back into my normal Sunday routine. Getting up; going to Sunday morning service; cooking dinner; and watching the "idiot box" the rest of the evening or it was watching me. One night the phone rang at 2:00 a.m. I sat straight up in bed, hoping and praying it was Steve, thinking he was ready to come over and talk things through. I couldn't believe whose voice I heard-it was Brian! I had not spoken with him in almost a year. He said he woke up out of a sound sleep and he wanted to tell me that he loved me and that he wanted to start afresh. He swore that he was no longer using drugs and he wanted his family back. He used the same old line that he had used before. He was like the little boy who cried wolf! I let Brian finish his well prepared speech. Steve had really changed my life and way of thinking. I had become use to the finer things of life and for me to lower myself and fall back into a relationship with Brian would be beneath me. For the next couple of weeks, Brian continued to use his suave and charm to persuade me to at least let him come and visit for the weekend.

Brian arrived a few days later. It was strange being with him again. We seemed so different now. The next day was Sunday and we went to Bishop Jenkins' Church. During the altar call, Brian, surprisingly, went down to the altar to give his life to the Lord and he was baptized in the name of the Lord. Amazingly, I thought, I had not mentioned anything to Brian about giving his life to the Lord. I tried to rejoice in the Lord, but I couldn't. Every Sunday, I paid my tithes and gave good offerings. Pastor Lewis was very fond of me and he never gave me any indication that he was concerned that I was struggling spiritually. I began to feel that the Lord knew my heart and all I wanted was a family; a husband so that I would not live in sin. Since 1986, I had been praying for this day to come. Brian was no longer my husband. I just didn't understand why things happened the way they did sometimes.

Brian's weekend visit turned into an extended stay. He went out and found a job. In his mind, I was still his wife, so he paid his fair share of the bills. Nothing sexual happened between us. Once, we tried to be intimate, but I was completely turned off.

One snowy Saturday night, Mrs. Henderson called me to say Steve wanted to bring his son, Anthony, over to play with Brian Jr. This was definitely not a good time. I had to make up a lie and tell her that Anthony would have to come some other time, because Steve could not know that I had let Brian come back. He would think I was a very weak woman, so I wanted to avoid him finding out.

Brian's salvation was very short lived. Within a few days of his repentance, he was back to staying out all night on payday and smoking crack. No way in the world was I going to let him back into my home. He had to go today-not next week-today! Brian gave me a song and dance about how no one cared about him or loved him. I told him Jesus does, but you've gotta get out of my house, brother. It was too good to be true, the devil is always trying new tricks on me.

One man after another entered my life. There was Bill, the Barber; Cortez, the Smooth Operator; Rick, the other Barber; John, the Faking Preacher. I asked the Lord what the problem was; why couldn't I have a husband? What is so wrong with me wanting to do the right thing? The Lord said that marriage is honorable and all, but apparently that did not apply to me. It seemed so unfair. Everyone seemed to be getting married; happily enjoying married life, while I was left being a single parent and trying to live a Christian life, but it seemed as though things could not come together for me. I had tried everything that I could think of and no one was working out for me.

Gwendolyn Jackson

One of my company affiliates was located in Northern Virginia, near Washington D.C. A supervisor in my unit called me one day to get information regarding the way we handled a procedure in the St. Louis office. After talking awhile, we became very comfortable with one another. Later I found out that he was a born again Christian. Joshua was his name. Within a week or so, he had mailed me tapes from his church. One of the messages was "Fighting and Winning Battles". I was so excited to make a spiritual connection with a male counterpart. Before I knew it, things had become very serious. Joshua wanted to meet me in person and offered to buy me a plane ticket to come for a weekend visit. My American Express card had been maxed out and he paid it off! I was really impressed. Born again; spirit-filled and, he was from West Africa-part of a wealthy family. I had hit the jackpot!

When it rains, it pours. Now Steve and I had gotten back on speaking terms. I managed to get tickets for a Forty Niners' game in San Francisco. Steve and I headed west for a long weekend. He had brought his golf clubs and we just enjoyed ourselves, visiting many sites I remembered. We went to Oakland, Alameda, Pier 39 and across the Golden Gate Bridge to Sausalito. While we were in Oakland, we got baseball tickets to see the Oakland A's. Baseball and football all in one weekend! The commercial for the Fog City Diner had been on TV back home and we went there for lunch. On the door, there was a sign that read, "No Cry Babies", which to me meant that if you can't afford to eat here, don't come in. But the food was good and the prices were reasonable. To close out our great weekend, Steve and I had a very romantic dinner at Charlie Brown's at The Fisherman's Wharf. We had a serious conversation that night. Steve told me that he knew that I wanted to be married, but at that point in his life, he was too selfish and stingy to marry anyone. Steve told me that he needed to sow his wild oats. I was so disappointed because I knew without a doubt that we would be a dynamic duo together, but I could not make this man want to marry me. I gracefully bowed out and told him that I

Thy Maker Is Thy Husband

hoped we could remain friends for a lifetime. He said that I would always be Ms. T to him, a very special lady. Steve often told me that I was a real lady. That really made me feel good. At least our last time together was a special one which I will always remember. We arrived back in St. Louis, said our good byes and promised to keep in touch with one another and we went our separate ways. Inside, I felt pretty sad, but I knew I had to let him go.

While I was away on my weekend, a high school friend, Denise and her three-year-old daughter, were killed by her boyfriend. This left me in a state of total shock. Denise reminded me so much of myself. She too, wanted to be loved and was searching. Now the search had taken her life and that of her three-year-old baby. Why? Two years ago, Denise and her daughter came to visit me at church. I had run into her at the drug store and invited her. She briefly told me that she was divorced. She had been beaten by her ex-husband and abused by her daughter's father. Denise just wanted to be loved and to have the peace of God in her life. I knew that her mother and sister were involved in the church, but Denise had never made a total commitment. I began to have flashbacks of all the times we had spoken and the things that she had shared with me. I was so caught up in my own life, that I lost touch with her after she had tried to re-dedicate her life to God. I was sick. All her friends from high school got together and went to her funeral. I cried and cried. Her ex-husband was there and he could hardly take it. I heard that had he been a good husband, she would not have been with the boyfriend and gotten killed. Bishop Sterns preached a message that I wouldn't soon forget. He was talking to us young people that day. We were between the ages of twenty-six to twenty-seven and we had seen one of our fellow classmates' life get taken away by a man. After the funeral, we all got together and reflected on life. We had a wake up call.

The following week, I had plane tickets to go and meet Joshua. Maybe it was good that it worked out that way; it took my mind off Denise. I asked the Lord to keep my desire from becoming tragic. I wanted to do what was right and I hoped the Lord would have patience and mercy.

Joshua and I had no idea who we were looking for at the airport, but we managed to spot each other right away. My friend, Loretta, who worked with Joshua had only said nice things about him and she told me that everyone at the company loved him. This man had a dozen long stem red roses in the trunk of his car for me-tied with a red bow. Joshua took me to my motel room and from behind his back he pulled out another gift. A complete perfume collection, including body lotions, powders. I knew that I was going to be treated like a queen this weekend. We had dinner plans with Loretta and her husband. Loretta was anxious to hear what I thought of Joshua. I told her that I was very impressed and he was starting off on the right foot. Dinner was lovely and the entire weekend was fantastic. Joshua took me shopping and bought me anything that I asked for. He also bought gifts for Brian Jr.. I felt like royalty. At the end of our second date, as Joshua was ready to leave, I grabbed him by the arm and passionately kissed him. From that point on, I had him in the palm of my hand. If I said jump, all he wanted to know was how high he should jump. He was sprung!

Now Thanksgiving had rolled around and Joshua had decided that he wanted to come and visit me in St. Louis and meet my family. Joshua was eleven years older than me, so I was a little apprehensive about my family meeting him. Again, Joshua was as charming as he was when I met him the first time. Whether Joshua knew this or not, the way to an American woman's heart is through the shopping mall. He certainly captured my family's heart. Joshua bought us all gifts. He said it was the custom in his country. We took them well-no problem at all!

Joshua had a long talk with my father. He told him that he wanted to marry me and take my back to the East Coast. Now this was pretty shocking. I was not expecting him to say anything like that. Joshua and I had only known each other via telephone for a few months. Things were moving almost too fast for me! Joshua had a field day schmoozing my family. He had won their hearts. By Christmas Day, Joshua had sent a beautiful diamond marquise engagement ring and asked me to marry him and move to Virginia. A thousand thoughts were going through my mind. I heard voices saying, "Now here's your chance. You'd better take it, or it may be your last." Before I knew it, I had said yes. In a matter of a few weeks, my life had changed. I turned in my notice at the best paying job I would ever have; gave up my catering business; pulled my son out of school-heading for the East Coast. My friends and family thought I had lost my mind for sure. I called Steve and Ms. Henderson to let them know that we were moving East. Ms. Henderson was really hurt and Steve was in a state of shock. This was enough for Steve to pay me a visit. Steve was looking at me as though I had lost all my marbles. I just told him that I had to make a move. I didn't tell him, but he was partly to blame for my quick decision. Tommy called me from San Diego and put his two cents in. Quoting scriptures and carrying on. Tommy kept telling me to make sure that I had heard from the Lord. This was my life and I had to do what was best for me and Brian Jr. Joshua loved us and wanted to make a life with us.

Joshua had made arrangements for the van lines to move all of our things and my car. Joshua had bought tickets for us to fly on Eastern Airlines and the day we left was their last day of business. I mean this was the worst airplane I had ever taken. When Joshua arrived at the airport, he greeted me with bad news. The money that he was waiting for did not come, so he didn't have the money to pay for the truck when it arrived with my things. Not good, I thought. I ended up having to call home to borrow money to pay for the truck. When his money finally came, I had to go off on him to get money to pay back what had been borrowed. Job hunting was pretty slow; the area was so big and the people drove wildly, just like in California. The townhouse that Joshua got for us was a gorgeous-three bedrooms; two and a half baths; a beautiful sun deck; and my most prized and sought after luxuries-a washer and dryer. I thought I had it going on for sure.

I started a job at an insurance company twenty-five miles from where we lived. I was scared of having to go that far to work in a strange city, but I had to work somewhere. I missed the family back home, but things weren't too bad as I got into my routine. Every evening, after work, Brian Jr. and I would walk up the street and get the mail. One day Joshua happened to have a letter from his parents in West Africa. When Joshua arrived home from work, I gave him the letter. He sat down and read the letter and got very quiet. He told me that his parents got word that he was going to marry an American girl and that if he did, he would be banished from the family. Without blinking his eyes, he told me that we could not get married because he could not betray his family. I immediately went ballistic. I snapped, went completely off the deep end. I had only been there for three weeks. I had quit my job, closed up my catering business, moved out of my home and come clear across the country for this?! Oh no, brother, you will not do me like this.

At that point, I wasn't thinking about God, or anything else. Joshua's life was on the line. I told him he had better pray that he woke up in the morning because I just may cut his throat. And the scary thing about that was that I meant It! For an entire month, I did not say one word to him. I was so bitter and angry, I could hardly function. Going to work everyday was my therapy. I managed to fool the people there. They had no idea that anything was going on at all. After a month or so, I finally broke the silence; I could not let this situation get the better of me. I told Joshua that he had broken my heart and that my life was a complete mess again! And Joshua tried his best to comfort me, but there was nothing that he could say or do to make things better. To make matters worse, I found out that Joshua had an estranged wife whom he had brought with him from Africa. He kept her confined to her apartment, thinking that immigration would not find out that she was in this country illegally. She had nearly lost her mind from what I had heard from Joshua, he said

Thy Maker Is Thy Husband

it was something genetic that caused her mental problems, but I believe he probably drove that woman crazy.

I threatened to call the immigration department on him and tell them he was hiding an illegal immigrant and that nearly sent him over the edge. I decided not to be that cold-blooded (even though he deserved it after what he had done to me). I believed in my heart of hearts that Joshua wooed, wined and dined me just to get something he wanted really bad, to marry an American to get his family over to this country. I let Joshua know that hell would freeze over twice before I would ever forgive him for makings a total mess of my life.

As the weeks passed, the resentment slowly diminished. The D.C. area was a very exciting place to live, but I couldn't afford to stay there alone with Brian Jr. After talking things over with my family, we all decided that it would be best for me to move back to St. Louis. Joshua just didn't know how much danger he had put himself in. At one point, I had thought about calling some of the home boys that I knew were notorious street gang members to smoke him for what he had done to me. Thank God, I didn't go completely crazy.

My last morning in D.C., I went outside on the deck and just stared into the sky. I asked the Lord what was wrong with me. Time after time I kept getting myself into bad situations and each situation seems to get more serious. This was all because I wanted to be loved and have a husband. I had been told time and time again, to seek first the Kingdom of God and all His righteousness and all of these things will be added to you. I just cried out and asked God to put my life back together again.

Martise's flight from St. Louis was scheduled to land at Washington National Airport at 5:15 p.m. Joshua agreed to go with me to pick him up and show him a little bit of the nation's capitol before driving back to St. Louis the next day. Joshua pulled Martise to the side and called himself making an apology to the family for this major disappointment. Later that night, Joshua and I sat up and talked until the wee hours of the morning. Joshua swore to me that I was not part of any conspiracy to get his family into the United States. He told me that he really loved me and Brian Jr. He was sorry things had turned out the way they had. I had no choice but to accept his apology and move on with my life. We fell asleep together on the floor. This would be the very last time we would spend the night together and we made the best of it.

The next morning, Joshua stood weeping on the front steps of the townhouse as we got ready to leave. We both knew that we had a time of chastisement and repenting in the sight of God. Some way, some how, we knew that the Lord was going to work things out for our good. Martise, Brian Jr. and I hugged Joshua good bye and we drove away.

CHAPTER 7

TRICK OR TREAT

The beauty of the countryside was something to behold as we drove back to St. Louis. God made everything so color coordinated, I realized. Out west, are the pretty orange, red and brown colors of the desert; passing through the Midwest, is the yellow of wheat crops. Approaching the East Coast are the beautiful green trees of the Appalachian Mountains. God is truly amazing.

Martise tried to keep me in good spirits as we drove back. I wanted him to think I was doing fine, despite everything that had happened. But deep down inside, I was really afraid. I didn't have a dime to my name- no job; no place to live. When I got back to St. Louis, I knew that I would have to go to the Division of Family Services to apply for assistance. Just a couple of years ago, I was living large. It was time for me to sell out completely to the Lord. I had known better before I ever went to Virginia, but I let the devil steal my lunch again. The Lord's patience was growing thin. This time I would pay dearly for my transgression. ***"Correction is grievous unto him that forsaketh the way: and he that hateth reproof shall die." (Proverbs 15:10)*** I knew the Lord and I was heading straight to the potter's house. The Lord told me that it was time for me to grow up. He was sick and tired of me falling into sin and making excuses for my actions. He told me that I was getting ready for a ride on the potter's wheel. Then I was going into the oven to burn up all the junk inside me. After cooling off for a short while, I would be put back into the oven, not to come out until the Lord finished with me, pure as gold, or until I died. It was as though the Lord was giving me an ultimatum. "Either you are going to live for me and allow me to use you for My service and My glory, or I am going to spit you out of my mouth." There were no ifs ands, or buts, about it-the Lord was upset with me. I felt as though I had broken His heart. Once again, I fell to my knees crying and repenting to the Lord, but this time it was different. Without a doubt I knew better, but it was though I had lost complete control of my emotions and I couldn't resist the temptations of my flesh. Only the Lord would be able to deliver me. For a very long time, I tried to use self control-I failed. I knew I had some tough days ahead and I knew that the Lord would see me through, but I was going to have to submit my complete will to Him.

Because the Lord is good all the time, He had mercy upon me once again. Within a few weeks, I got a pretty good position at a managed care company. It was a blessing that I did not have to stay on family assistance for very long. Within a couple of months, I was promoted and my base salary was just a little below what I had been making before I left St. Louis last year. Slowly, but surely, God was making everything come together. It took a lot of fasting and prayer on my behalf. There were plenty of opportunities for me to slip again, but I was determined to make it this time.

Brian came by to visit Brian Jr. one afternoon. We thought it would be nice to go out, get pizza, bring it back to the house and sit and visit for awhile. As we were driving to get the pizza, I noticed a very strange smell on Brian, like burnt trash or something. I asked him what it was and he said he didn't know what I was talking about. He really smelled bad. Brian kept coughing as we drove along. By the time we got back with the pizza, he could hardly sit up at the table to eat the pizza. Brian rushed into the bedroom and literally fell across the bed and started grabbing his chest. I yelled, asking what was the matter? He said "Denise! I can't breathe!"

"Oh my God!" I cried, "It's the crack! It's about to kill you!" Without even thinking to call 911, I managed to get him into the car and put Brian Jr. in the back seat. I drove like crazy to the emergency room. The emergency room staff rolled him into the examination room immediately. An incision was made on the upper side of his rib cage and they inserted some sort of tube through the incision to try and pump his lungs. The crack had caused his lungs to collapse. Once Brian was stabilized, the emergency room doctor told me that if I had I waited another fifteen minutes to get him to the hospital, he would have died. A chill went down my back as I thought about what the doctor had just said. I tried to call Mrs. Williams, but she was out of town visiting Carla in Dallas. I was able to reach Shirley, Brian's older sister, to let her know what had happened to him. I couldn't seem to get this man off my back. All I tried to do was be nice and let him come by to eat pizza with his son and I ended up in the emergency room with him half dead. My life was a never ending soap opera, except I couldn't change the channel when I got sick of all the melodrama. I asked the Lord why it was taking so long for Brian to be delivered from crack cocaine. More than six years had passed since I had first prayed that the Lord deliver him. I can remember when all of the brothers and sisters in the Lord that I associated with, would fellowship and we would have intervention prayers just for Brian. But instead of being delivered from this terrible drug, he seemed to be getting worse. At this point, I just didn't understand what was going on in his life anymore.

Having just gotten out of a terrible situation myself, I didn't have the time or the energy to try to preach to Brian any longer. I really had to concentrate on myself, for the Word of God clearly states, ***"Thou hypocrite, first cast out the beam out of thine own eye; then shalt thou see clearly to cast out he mote out of thy brother's eye." (Matthew 7:5)*** For years, I had been slipping and dipping. Pretending to be so holy and such a spirit filled believer, I had been deceiving myself. It was time to be real and I had to stop playing with fire-or sooner or later I was going to be burned.

Martise, Louise and I drove down to Oklahoma for the church anniversary service of one of our favorite preachers. Evangelist Charles Pruitt was a profound man of God. I knew that I would hear a word from the Lord on this trip. The theme of this meeting was the "Perfection' of Divine Order" – just what

I needed in my life right now. In the past nine years, I had probably moved at least a dozen times and been in and out of numerous relationships. I was sick and tired of all the instability in my life. My life was in desperate need of divine order and God was going to do just that if I allowed Him to.

For three days, I had a little bit of heaven on earth. The glory of the Lord was in that place. Everything–the music, the praise and worship, the preaching-was beautiful. The Lord was being worshipped in that place in the beauty of holiness for sure. After being revived, refreshed and renewed in my spirit, it was time to head home. For the first time in a long while, I knew and felt that God was with me. I also knew that I had no margin for error, because God was getting ready to use me for his service. I realized that I had a calling since I was sixteen years old and had been running from that calling ever since. It was time to stop running from the Lord, because I saw that I couldn't win the race.

On my job, I was promoted to supervisor and my catering business was starting to pick up again. Pastor Lewis had asked me about becoming part of the leadership at our church, but I really wanted to seek the Lord for confirmation. This time I didn't want to let Pastor Lewis or the Lord down. The thought of having a male companion started to become less important to me. I tried to focus my affections on things above and not earthly things. My spirit felt so free knowing that I had nothing to be ashamed of any longer. It was a different feeling from when I was living the life of a carnal Christian. No more chains were holding me down.

Our store, down in the city, closed for two hours every afternoon. Brian Jr. would ride to open the store back up with my mother; and I would pick him up each evening. As I was waiting for him one afternoon, my old boyfriend, Brandon, pulled up. I was so surprised to see him. We greeted one another with a holy hug and he told me that he and his wife had been called to Pastor a church. Brandon said that it was one of the most difficult things that he had ever done. Brandon went on

Thy Maker Is Thy Husband

to tell me that his congregation more or less betrayed him and his wife and he left that ministry. The Lord had led them to move to Oklahoma to go to Bible College and join up with a new ministry. Brandon wanted to know if I had ten or twenty dollars. He was really stretching out on faith. He and his wife were trying to raise gas and food money to make their journey to Oklahoma. I felt compelled to give him what I had, because he had enough faith and courage to make a move like that. I could remember when Brandon didn't know the Lord and now the Lord had called him to pastor. But the Lord uses the least of us. And makes us greater and mightier men and women for his service.

As Brian Jr. and I were riding down the street singing praises unto the Lord, two young men were driving next to me trying to flirt. At first I ignored them, but then I thought it would be a good opportunity to witness to them. I rolled down my window and they both said, "How are you doing today young lady?"

"Blessed," was my response.

Both of the young men looked at each other, as if to say, "Oh man, she's one of those church women." I could see them carrying on a conversation as we stopped at the traffic light. As we started to pull off, the young man on the passenger's side asked me what my name was and I told him, "Denise Turner." He told me that his name was Carlos Fitzpatrick. Very dignified name, I thought to myself. I asked him if he was trusting Jesus. He sort of looked strangely and said, "Well, of course I am." As I pulled off, I told them to be blessed and keep trusting God. I looked up into my rearview mirror and it appeared as though they were following me. Another red light stopped me and Carlos wanted to know if he could give me a call sometime. My response, "No, I don't talk to strangers." He sort of laughed, as if he didn't take me seriously. As we continued driving down the street, Carlos asked for my phone number one last time and I handed him one of my business cards through the window.

For several days, Carlos tried to reach me, leaving messages on my machine at home and voice mail messages at work. I had been on such a spiritual high lately, that I didn't want anything or anyone to interfere with it. Finally, I decided to go ahead and give him a call. Carlos was very surprised to hear from me and told me that he didn't think I was going to call. He wanted to take me out to dinner, but he had the same problem so many brothers have-no car!! Well, he had a car, but it wasn't running. I felt strange picking him up, without really knowing anything about him. Carlos lived with his cousin, who was a police officer, so that made me feel a little more comfortable about picking him up for our date. To my surprise, he looked very different than he did the first time we met.

He didn't talk very much at first, but, as we were riding along, he began to open up. We were telling each other a little bit about our past, present and what we would like to do in our future. We ate at a restaurant that was famous for its ribs. I wasn't sure if our date was Dutch or not, so I came prepared to pay. However, Carlos ended up paying the whole bill. After we finished, we rode down the road listening to some nice jazz. I told Carlos that I only listened to gospel and jazz. Some love songs were O.K. too, I told him. He was into that crazy rap, listening to Ice Cube, Ice T and all those people who sing that crazy stuff. He really didn't seem like that kind of guy, but I guess you can't judge a book by its cover. I told Carlos that the next relationship that God blessed me with, would be with a Godly man, that I was tired of compromising for less. Holy Ghost boldness came upon me. I wasn't concerned about what he thought about my Godly convictions. He began to tell me how he had been wanting a Godly woman in his life for a very long time. That he needed a woman who could help lead him back in the right direction. He admitted to me that he really wanted to get his life back in order with God. It was nice to have a male friend who didn't mind talking about the Lord. We decided to stop at the video store and rent a couple of movies to wind up our first date. When we arrived back at my house, my mother was waiting to check him out. Carlos was very nervous about meeting my mother. He had hoped to make a good

Thy Maker Is Thy Husband

impression. NOT! I don't know what he was thinking. Even I wasn't too impressed with what he was wearing. The first thing my mother noticed were these strange looking jeans with a woman painted on them. She was cordial nevertheless. We sat in the kitchen and made small talk. Mother told Carlos that he looked like a football player. He laughed and told her he played football in high school and that he had a chance for a college scholarship, but family problems didn't allow that to happen. I picked up right then that that was a touchy subject with him. Later, we went on up to my living quarters where he and Brian Jr. got to know each other.

A few weeks passed and things were going pretty well with Carlos and I. He and Brian Jr. were getting along very well. I had a hard time in the past finding someone that my son actually liked. Carlos and I spent time together almost daily after we met. He seemed like a very nice young man. He wasn't moving too fast, he respected me a lot and he wanted to rededicate his life to the Lord. His cousin moved out of the apartment they shared and some old friends of his moved in. I wasn't too thrilled at the idea of him rooming with these old friends, because they seemed like they could be trouble for him, but it seemed like he had everything under control. Carlos had a nice job at one of the car plants here in the city. He made very nice money and someday wanted to have a family. That began to catch my attention. As a matter of fact, Carlos went on to tell me that the very next day after we met, he told his grandmother that I was going to be the woman he married. He said his grandmother laughed at him. Carlos had the reputation of being a player, a ladies' man. He had told his family that he would never get married. Now, all of a sudden, he was singing a different tune. I asked Carlos what made him say something like that, but he said he didn't know himself. He just knew that I was the one. Things between Carlos and I began to get very serious. I was determined not to fall back into a sin trap again, but Carlos and I spent a lot of time alone and we became that much closer.

Gwendolyn Jackson

It was nice, cool summer evening, Carlos' birthday and I wanted to do something special for him. I grilled steaks, bought a special cake and a small, but special birthday gift for him. Carlos, Brian Jr. and I shared this special evening together. After dinner, Brian Jr. fell asleep and Carlos began to tell me how special I made him feel; and that he was falling for me. Carlos said that I was the first woman that made him feel this way and we hadn't even made love yet. The next thing I knew, Carlos and I got passionate, then it happened-the thing I feared the most-falling into the sin trap of fornication. I couldn't seem to control my flesh. From that day on, it became a regular part of our relationship. Just as in times past, my relationship with my Heavenly Father began to grow cold, but I continued to go to church, fast, pray and read the word. I knew that if I just stopped doing everything that the devil would really take control.

Carlos was very good to Brian Jr. and me. He gave me practically everything I wanted. He would give me his check every Friday to pay my bills, just as if I was his wife. I was loving every minute of it. One thing, that still bothered me, was his roommates. I had a feeling that something was going on there that wasn't quite right. His homeboys didn't like me at all. They would tease Carlos, saying all those ugly things that guys say to each other, but I really didn't care what they thought of me. His homeboys would make fun of him going to Boy Scout meetings with Brian Jr. I would come right back and tell them if he runs with me he's going to be alright, but if he keeps hanging out with you bums, he's going to end up in the penitentiary. Carlos would get upset every time I said that, but it was the truth.

We were in revival at our church. An evangelist had flown in from Southern California to minister. One thing about it, I knew better than to stop fellowshipping with other believers, so I continued to go to church faithfully each and every Sunday. Carlos had started going with me pretty regularly also. The evangelist spoke some very powerful words that really hit home. Just the night before, I had been reading in my Bible the book of Revelation where Jesus was telling the Church of Pergamos that

Thy Maker Is Thy Husband

He had a few things against them. The evangelist read that exact same scripture! That really struck me. The Lord was talking straight to me. I just couldn't understand why I couldn't be delivered in this area. During the service I cried to myself and asked why couldn't I be delivered?

The days and months following started a change in my life. God knew that I wanted to be delivered. I was always told be careful what you pray for-you just may get it! The Lord was even dealing with Carlos. We went to church with my brother, Martise and his family. Carlos was being ministered to. He was even shedding tears because the word of God was so powerful in the service. God was pulling and drawing him, but Carlos just didn't want to surrender all. I wanted so badly for Carlos to go down and give his life to the Lord. I knew we could live a life together that was pleasing in the sight of the Lord, but it didn't happen. Carlos told me in the car, he almost went down, but he was too shy to get up in front of all the people. I told him that shouldn't have mattered, because everyone had to do it at sometime or another.

One night, Carlos was supposed to pick me up at eight o'clock for a date. We were really starting to bond and build a relationship, or so I thought. I fell asleep laying on the bed waiting; and the next thing I knew, it was eleven thirty. I jumped up and immediately began paging him, but he never called back. I paged him at least fifteen times, with no answer. Oh, my God, I thought, he's been smoked running with those hoodlums in the streets. I panicked; I called his homeboy, "Q", who told me to calm down, he had been trying to page him too, but wasn't getting an answer. That wasn't like Carlos at all. We had been together almost twenty four/seven and if not together, just a phone call away. Finally, after another hour, Carlos called. I yelled, "Why didn't you answer my pages?"

He said, "Baby, I am in jail out in the county." My heart skipped a beat. The walls came tumbling down, the party was over. Carlos had been charged with selling crack cocaine to an undercover narcotics detective. His so-called associates had just caused his life to come to a screeching halt. The Lord had been trying to tell Carlos to come to him, but he hadn't listened.

Just two weeks ago, Carlos had been driving my car with an expired drivers' license. Thinking that he would go to jail for not having a license he had sped away from the police chasing him and crashed my car into a concrete barrier–completely totaling my car. Initially, the insurance was not going to pay and the appraiser said the car couldn't be repaired. It was a terrible situation, but God, who is rich and merciful, allowed the insurance company to have a change of heart and repair my car; and Tony's Body Shop was able to bring my car back from the grave. We both sat outside just a few days before this night realizing that God was sending a warning through the car accident, not even allowing Carlos to get one scratch. But we didn't take heed. I was afraid. I knew something was going to happen, but I just wasn't sure what. The Lord kept speaking judgment, judgment and judgment to you. Now, Carlos was in jail.

That next morning I called Carlos' lawyer and we went to see if we could post bail for him. His bail was set at two hundred fifty thousand dollars! He was stuck there where no one could help him. His lawyer spoke with another judge, who thought Carlos' bail was ridiculously high and he dropped it to thirty five thousand dollars. Before Carlos' grandmother posted bond for him, a thought entered my mind. Could it be that the Lord was trying to save us from ourselves? Could it be that the Lord was trying to sit Carlos down before matters got worse? Nevertheless, we got ourselves out of another jam-so we thought.

The holidays were quickly approaching once again. All of the family was heading south to Arkansas for our cousin's wedding. We were all looking forward to this gala event. My family was getting used to Carlos and he was invited to go along to the wedding. We rode with my parents and aunt. They all warmed up to him pretty quickly. I was fantasizing, pretending to be already married. Carlos was everything I ever dreamed of

Thy Maker Is Thy Husband

having in a husband. We were just one big happy family on a late fall vacation. But just as my family was beginning to accept Carlos as being my significant other, it soon became obvious that we were as different as night and day.

Carlos was facing great uncertainty. Catching a drug case was the last thing he needed, especially with all of the inequities in the judicial system that are geared towards enslaving our young black men. Secondly, Carlos had just recently been paroled, which I found out after I fell for him. From what I understood, it didn't look good at all, to be on parole and catch another case. Carlos had been incarcerated for three years for stealing. He and his brother had been caught stealing clothes from the department store they worked in. He couldn't deny the fact that he was guilty as sin, so he went ahead and took responsibility for his actions. It was not my intent at all to get hooked up with and ex-con, but it was too late now to turn back. I had really fallen in love with him. Carlos said this trip to Arkansas was his first real family trip.

I didn't understand how I had attracted all of these wounded, hurting men. Carlos' father was extremely abusive to Carlos' mother-a twenty five year old with eight children. His mother left him and seven other sibling at the welfare office when Carlos was only two years old, with his father's work number and social security number written on a piece of paper in the pocket of the oldest child. She knew no other way out but to break and run. The eight children were split up, with the four boys going to live with their father and eventually, the four girls with their mother. Carlos and his brothers had several stepmothers, who eventually left them because of the abuse they suffered as well. Carlos and his brothers were physically, verbally and mentally abused by their father. He would try to win them back by buying their love with material things. That was the only way he knew to show them love.

Carlos was a very gifted athlete and from what I had been told, had Carlos had the family stability that he needed, he would have definitely made it to the NFL. They say the boy was BAD!

Gwendolyn Jackson

After Carlos graduated from high school, which was a miracle in itself, considering his circumstances, he began to live life in the fast lane. He told me that he felt the world owed him something because of what he had suffered. So he took what he wanted by force. Whether it was women, material possessions, whatever- he really didn't care. This attitude of "take it by force", resulted in his first visit to the Missouri Department of Corrections. But now I asked my self, Lord, why? How did I get involved with a man with so many problems? A man that has mental scars beyond your wildest dreams? How? I asked the Lord again. And the Lord answered me. Because of the lust of my flesh, I was spiritually dead. My flesh won the battle over my spirit and now, I had a mess on my hands.

As the New Year approached, Carlos and I were still holding on, but I knew something was going on with me spiritually. Even though I was living in sin, I started to seek the Lord once again. I had never felt this way before. There was a sense of constant terror upon me. It had gotten so bad that I was afraid to drive my car alone for fear of this unknown force. So I did everything possible to avoid being alone. I couldn't even identify what I was fearful of, but it was there and it was very real. Then I finally realized what I was afraid of. It was God. I reminded myself of Adam when he was in the garden and the Lord said to Adam, ***"Where are thou?" And then Adam responded by saying, "I heard thy voice in the garden and I was afraid, because I was naked; and I hid myself." (Gen. 3:9-10)*** Just as Adam had been afraid of God's impending judgment, so was I. I knew I had gone too far. This time I felt I had broken the very heart of God; I became very displeasing in his sight.

It was time for Mother Nature to visit me once again. Normally she is on time like clock work. I had stopped taking birth control pills shortly after Carlos caught the drug case. I had fallen for him so hard, that I didn't want to think about not having him with me, so actually I quit taking the pill on purpose, hoping to get pregnant. And I got just what I asked for. After two weeks, I bought a home pregnancy kit, rushed home from

Thy Maker Is Thy Husband

work to take the test and the blue line was there. We hit the Bull's Eye! I couldn't wait for Carlos to come home to tell him. I was waiting at the front door for him and I gently pulled him over to the sofa and said, "Congratulations, Dad!"

He responded by saying, "Who are you talking to?"

I said, "You, silly!" Carlos was in a state of shock.

CHAPTER 8

STORMY WEATHER

Carlos, Brian Jr. and I took our first trip to the obstetrician to confirm the pregnancy. Carlos was still in denial. I was fine, except for being sleepy all the time. Meanwhile, Carlos was throwing up and having morning sickness. It was pretty weird. Dr. Martinez said I was definitely with child and that my due date was October 20th. Reality hit home! I was having a baby with a man that I wasn't married to. I kept thinking how disappointed Pastor Richards was going to be with me. Pastor Debbie had so much confidence and faith in me. Until now, I had been able to hide from him what was in my closet. The Lord assures us in His word that, ***"If ye will not do so, behold ye have sinned against the Lord; and be sure your sin will find you out" (Numbers. 32:32).*** I knew everyone would be in a state of shock about my news. Everyone thought of me as Miss Goody Two Shoes. Denise was near perfect in everyone's eyes. I was always talking about the Lord and the word of God. I really loved the Lord, but I needed Deliverance.

Now, looking back in retrospect, I had never been healed or delivered from my first marriage and my quest to find another husband all resulted from the wounds and voids that I still had from Brian Sr. But I knew that no time was better than the present for me to be delivered. How much more damage could I do anyway? I knew God was drawing me and pulling me and this was where I stopped. I told Carlos that we couldn't continue living together. Either he would have to marry me, or we were going to have to go our separate ways. To my surprise Carlos didn't seem to have a problem with what I was saying. He turned and pulled me to him and said, "Denise, I knew you were going to be my wife from the day I saw you in traffic. All my life, I have been this wild man out of control, never treating any woman the way she deserved to be treated, but you were

Thy Maker Is Thy Husband

different. First of all, you were not going to let me treat you like that and secondly, I didn't want to treat you that way. You are a jewel and I don't even know if I deserve to have you as my wife, but I sure would like to. Denise, I want to marry you."

I was stunned! Carlos wanted to marry me right away! He wanted us to get married on the date we met, June 15th. So it became official, we were engaged. Carlos called his grandma to tell her the news. She was shocked! No one in his family ever thought he would be married. He was Daddy Mack; Don Juan; Casanova; player of all players. He had finally decided to settle down. His grandma said, "It's a miracle." Before I told anyone, I wanted to go and meet my pastors. I had already repented to the Lord, but I knew I still needed to go and confess my sin to them.

Pastor Lewis and Pastor Debbie were waiting for me in their office when I got to the church. I could tell by the look on their faces that they were very curious about the counseling session I had requested. This was one of the most difficult things that I had to do, especially since they had so much confidence and belief in me as they did. They both greeted me and told me to have a seat. I began to tell them the whole story about Carlos; about how I ended up in this compromising relationship, letting the enemy trick me into giving into the desires of my flesh. Tears began to flow; the Holy Spirit began to convict me. I was so happy that I was still able to be convicted. I continued to tell them about Carlos and his background, then finally I came with the blow. I told them that I was eight weeks pregnant. You could see the disappointment on their faces. But they were understanding and compassionate. They knew by my coming there, that I was sorry and that I knew that I had sinned against the Lord.

Pastor Lewis began to correct and rebuke me. The tears were really flowing now. Pastor Debbie began reading to me from Hebrews. The Lord was dealing with me in the manner in which a parent would deal with a child who had received a bad report card. The parent still loved the child dearly, but he/she still had to be punished for his/her behavior. Pastor Lewis and Pastor Debbie assured me that God still loved me just the same and they still loved me as well. They told me that when you compromise the principles of God, that things like this are certain to take place. The three of us held hands and they began to pray for me. Pastor Lewis laid his hands on my forehead and began to speak the word of God into my spirit. I knew from that moment that God was going to deliver me once and for all. I mean, he was praying fervently for me. Pastor Debbie then had a word from the Lord for me. She said, "The Lord said, *'Now glory be to God who by His mighty power at work within us is able to do far more than we would ever dare to ask or even dream of infinitely beyond our highest prayers, desires, thoughts, or hopes" (Ephesians 3:20).* I lost it at that point. I began to speak in other tongues and the anointing of God just fell on me in that office. The spirit of the Lord had not fallen upon me like that in months and God was about to do something new with me.

Carlos was waiting at the apartment when I got back. I spoke to him, but I didn't say anything else. When he broke the silence and asked how the meeting went, I told him "you should have come like I asked you to and then you'd know how it went." God was also dealing with Carlos, but he was running scared from the Lord. I had told Pastor Lewis that Carlos had asked me to marry him. Immediately Pastor Lewis said, "The Lord says not right now." I was really surprised. I thought getting married would be the right thing to do. I told Carlos what Pastor Lewis said about us getting married and that the Lord said we should wait. I learned from before that when the man of God gives you counsel, you had better listen or suffer the consequences. Carlos didn't have much to say after that. He jumped up off the couch and said he had to make a run. I was getting tired of him ripping and running the streets with those sorry friends of his. I kept telling him, those so called friends were going to cause him to have many lonely days, but he

Thy Maker Is Thy Husband

thought I just didn't like them. I told him, you will see one day who your friends are.

After work I thought I would stop by Mom and Dad's and bring them up to date. I told them that Carlos wanted to marry in June, but Pastor Lewis didn't feel that I should marry Carlos at this time. Of course, my mother agreed. She kept saying, it's just something strange about that boy, but she couldn't put her finger on what it was.

On Valentine's Day, Carlos and I had made special plans to go out. He did everything in a big way all the time. I was certain this would beat all of the Valentine Days of my past. We had dinner reservations for 4:30 p.m. At four o'clock, Carlos called to tell me he had to do something for his boy and he would be an hour or so late. By the time he arrived, it was 10:00 p.m.

I was hot as a firecracker! There was not enough explaining in the world to get him out of this one. I called him everything from a liar to a male prostitute. By the time I was finished going off, he was practically on the floor begging. I couldn't believe it! I had never been stood up on Valentine's Day by any man! That really took something out of me. It made me lose the respect and trust for Carlos that had taken me so long to get. I went to my room, slammed the door and didn't come out for the rest of the night. I laid in bed, just looking out of my window, with warm tears rolling down my face. Here I was pregnant with this man's child and he didn't have the decency to come and spend Valentine's Day with me. All men are dogs! This was the worst Valentine's Day I had ever had. I laid in bed staring out the window until I finally drifted off to sleep.

It was Monday morning and time to head off to work. Carlos dropped me off like he normally did. I had nothing to say to him. He kept saying baby, I'm sorry. I told him just drive me to work. I didn't want to hear his voice. My day stunk. All day long, people where asking how my Valentine's Day was. I just said it was O.K. I didn't want to let everyone know how big of a jerk Carlos had been. When I arrived home from work, I was so

Gwendolyn Jackson

sleepy that all I wanted to do was go to bed, but I had to spend some time with Brian Jr. and fix dinner. I walked into my bedroom and saw a dozen roses and a big white teddy bear. The card said how sorry he was for disappointing me. He was forever saying he was sorry for something. Why couldn't he just be responsible and do what he was supposed to do? I knew from the beginning that he would be a trip, but this was really more than I had bargained for.

The Valentine's Day disaster was behind us and we were thinking and preparing ourselves for our new baby. I still couldn't believe I was having a baby. It had been eight years. I had become convinced that it probably wouldn't happen again-mainly because I didn't have a husband. Another reason I wanted to be married so badly was that my biological clock was ticking away and I didn't want to be an old maid, having children. I dreaded the thought of having kids and being mistaken for the grandmother rather than the mother. Sometimes I would wonder and ask the Lord why am I having such a difficult time being single? This has been the most difficult thing that I have ever faced in my life. I wanted and needed answers desperately and I wasn't going to stop seeking the Lord for answers to my plight. One thing I never understood in the word of God was when the Apostle Paul made it seem almost appealing to be single. The only thing I can say about that is the apostle Paul was a bad brother. I just couldn't seem to fathom being single and satisfied. But I was going to find out, because I was tired of messing up my life. I was realizing that each time I made the same dumb mistakes in my relationships, it affected my son as well as me. Girlfriend had to get it together!

Thursday evening was TV night and Carlos and I loved to watch Martin Lawrence. Carlos would always say that Martin and Gina reminded him of us. I didn't think so, but I let him believe that. Carlos was always there on time to watch Martin, but was late tonight. I paged him, but got no answer. A funny feeling came over me and sure enough something was wrong

Thy Maker Is Thy Husband

again. Carlos called and he had been picked up and was being held on another drug charge.

This time I couldn't cry or laugh. I was in a state of shock. I was sure that I was going to wake up from this bad dream. It was as though I was in the eye of Hurricane Hugo and destruction was in my path. There was nothing that I could do and I wasn't sure if I wanted to do anything. I was sick and tired of all the chaos. Mentally, I knew I couldn't take much more. I felt as though the walls were closing in on me and that I was on the brink of an emotional breakdown or something.

The next thing I knew, Carlos was knocking at the door and he was scared to death. I had never seen him like that before. I asked him how he got out. He said the guard let him out by mistake. I told Carlos it was over. God had warned us and warned us. The party was over. For the next four days, Carlos and I remained in seclusion. I told him he had to go and turn himself back in. It was time to face the music; to deal with the consequences of his actions. The one thing Carlos decided to do before turning himself in, which I believed was the best thing he could do was give his life over to the Lord Jesus Christ. Carlos knew that he could not face what he was going to have to deal with alone. The words to this old gospel song came to life for us. If we ever needed the Lord, we sure do need him NOW. We went to service at Bishop Jenkins' church and he preached a very timely message that seemed to speak directly to the two of us. The title of his sermon was "Clean Me Up, Lord". Bishop Jenkins spoke from Psalms. Before Bishop Jenkins could finish reading the text, tears began to well up in Carlos' eyes. He remembered how God was dealing with him a few months ago when we went to church with Martise and now he realized that God was really trying to tell him something. Altar call was being made, the choir was singing softly, ministering in song, as the Pastor was offering the gift of eternal life. Carlos looked over at me and I said to him, you know what you need to do. Without hesitation, he walked down to the altar and gave his life to Jesus Christ and was baptized in the name of the Lord. This

Gwendolyn Jackson

was the first day of the rest of his new life. All at once, I felt as though we were going to make it through this storm.

The day of reckoning had come. Carlos, his brother, Donald, Mr. Peterson, his attorney and I drove to the county jail and Carlos turned himself back into the county department of justice . Carlos couldn't believe he was actually going to turn himself back in. We convinced him that in the long run, this was the best thing that he could have done for all of us. Of course, I didn't want him leaving being only ten weeks pregnant with our child, but I knew that it would only make matters worse for all of us. It was very difficult , but the Lord gave me a double portion of His strength and power. As a matter of fact, we didn't even shed a tear. I knew God was with us. I knew in my heart that this just wasn't for Carlos, but this was for me too. I was getting ready to go through my wilderness experience as well as Carlos.

The months and weeks passed; Carlos was still being held in the county jail awaiting trial. The pregnancy was going fine, but it hurt me at times that Carlos was not there with me to go to the doctor and to feel the baby moving in my stomach. But this was part of my wilderness. I was alone this time. Each Saturday, Brian Jr., I and my other family members would go out of the county jail and visit with Carlos. We could only stay an hour, behind the glass talking on the phone. This all was such a trip to me. I never thought I would be inside this place. Once, many years ago, Brian Sr. got picked up on a bench warrant for an outstanding traffic ticket and I had had to come and pay the ticket and pick him up. This was the real deal this time. Carlos' attorney, Mr. Peterson, said that Carlos could be faced with a lengthy prison sentence because he had two pending drug cases against him. Mr. Peterson was trying to convince Carlos that he should plea bargain and take the fifteen years the prosecuting attorney was offering. We both were terrified at the thought of him being in prison for fifteen years. So we said no to the fifteen year offer. Mr. Peterson thought we should have taken it. He said that African Americans rarely get light sentences in the county when they are convicted. But we told Mr. Peterson, that

Thy Maker Is Thy Husband

we believed that the Lord would allow us to be treated fairly and justly and we would go to trial, because God was with us.

It had been a long time since I had sought the face of the Lord as I was doing now. Each and everyday, I would go into prayer after I got home from work and cry out to the Lord for our situation, for our unborn child and for deliverance. I would pray and ask the Lord to keep our minds pure and to give us the strength we needed to endure this very serious trouble. I read every scripture in the word of God that spoke of God being with us in trouble. I was amazed that I was able to rest peacefully at night and still be pretty joyful during the day, despite my present situation. Everyday, I would read a passage from Psalms. One in particular, became my favorite because it promised what God would do when we were faced with trouble. The only thing we could do was to continue to depend on God. Carlos was continuing to grow daily in his Christian walk in the county jail. We wrote letters and shared scriptures with one another each day and he called if he was able to get to the telephone.

I was reminiscing, thinking this time last year we were celebrating Carlos' birthday together when I realized that he hadn't called. Much later, when he did, I noticed that the collect call had a different recording I hadn't heard before. They had moved him to a prison three hundred miles from home. All I could do was break down and cry. I asked him why they had moved him. He told me that it was due to him violating his parole and not reporting to his parole officer after he had been charged with a new offense. Carlos didn't realize that if he had gone to his parole officer that he could have avoided being in jail right now. So not only was I unable to see Carlos behind the glass each week, I wouldn't even be able to talk to him. The long distance collect calls would be too expensive with him being so far away. We had been praying and asking the Lord to help us and comfort us during this time, but things seemed to be getting worse instead of better. That was another powerful blow, but somehow we were able to brush off our knees and get back into the ring for the next round.

Mr. Peterson contacted me at work to let me know that Carlos' trial was going to begin. My heart dropped into my stomach. The future of our family would be in the hands of twelve men and women. It seemed like something straight from television. But it wasn't, this was really happening to us. Carlos and I had many conversations regarding the events that led to him being arrested. He swore to me that he hadn't sold the drugs to the police officer. He kept telling me that some other dude that he only knew by his street name, sold the drugs. He was out there, but he didn't do it. All I could do was believe him.

Carlos was brought back to the county jail a few days before his trial. As he was being taken to his cell, he saw the guy who he said sold the drugs to the cops. The two of them engaged in conversation and the guy agreed to talk to Mr. Peterson and tell him that he was the one who actually sold the drugs. We rejoiced and praised God for this taking place. We couldn't believe that he actually ran into this man. A lot of talking went back and forth between Carlos, Mr. Peterson and the other guy and his attorney. We later found out that the guy who supposedly sold the drugs was named Lee Jordan. Lee's attorney advised him that he shouldn't testify and admit to selling drugs to the police officer. So after all of the going back and forth, we weren't sure what was going to happen. All we could do was trust in God.

I was going into my ninth month. It was a miracle that I had done so well, under the circumstances. God had truly been with me. In the beginning of the pregnancy, I thought the stress from this ordeal was going to make me have a miscarriage, but God had other plans in mind for this child.

Carlos' trial was starting and I had a lot mixed emotions. Fear kept trying to creep in, but I kept remembering all that God had shown me and told me in the past months. I got down on my knees and prayed to the Lord. I asked him to give me the strength that I needed to make it through this week. I told Him no matter what happened, that I would still love Him and trust in Him. I believed that God only knew what was best for us; and

Thy Maker Is Thy Husband

our lives were in His hands. The Lord then led me to read *Psalms 112:5-7*. After reading that scripture, my stomach felt like the bottom had just fallen out of it. Nevertheless, I had to keep believing that the Lord was holding my hand and that he was more than able to keep me from falling.

My mother and I arrived at the county courthouse. It was the most eerie feeling I had ever had. I had never felt so helpless in all my life. In reality, there was nothing the lawyer, my mother, or anyone else could do to help us today. Our lives were hanging in the balance and our fate was about to be decided during the next few days. The guards brought Carlos to the courthouse from the county jail. I brought him very conservative clothing to wear for his court appearances. When Carlos walked into the courtroom, he looked so distinguished, no one would ever have thought that he was the defendant. Mr. Peterson took his seat next to Carlos and they spoke before the session began.

The judge entered the courtroom and the proceedings began. As the jury passed by, I couldn't believe my eyes. One of the supervisors I worked with had been selected as an alternate juror! Lord, I said to myself, everyone at work will know and now I'll probably lose my job! Things were not starting out too well. When I told Carlos' attorney that I knew one of the jurors, he said it didn't really matter, because she was an alternate. But it did matter-my reputation and character was on trial right along with Carlos'.

The prosecuting attorney began. She seemed like a pretty nice lady, but she was determined to send Carlos to prison because she despised drug dealers. She told the jury that Carlos was a murderer, because he sold poison to people on the streets and because of people like him, their children could not go outside to play. My heart was bleeding for him as she continued to cut him down like a lumberjack with a high-powered saw. By the time she finished, she had grounded him to saw dust. But even after those harsh accusations had been made against him, he was able to still hold his head high.

Gwendolyn Jackson

Mr. Peterson proceeded to present his defense for Carlos. He was very conservative, not a flashy, loud-mouthed attorney. He had a personal concern for Carlos and me and he told us that he was going to give this case everything he had. Mr. Peterson's style was very methodical and systematic. He refuted every negative statement that Ms. Lombardo made against Carlos and encouraged the jury to come to their own conclusion concerning Carlos Fitzpatrick's character and his innocence in the charges being brought against him.

The trial went on for four days and finally, Carlos' fate would be decided. All of the evidence had been presented. Lee Jordan had even come and testified that he had actually sold the drugs to the undercover detective and not Carlos. Mr. Peterson felt pretty confident that Carlos would be acquitted because of that key testimony. Ms. Lombardo and Mr. Peterson both did their final closing arguments. During Ms. Lombardo's closing arguments, I left the courtroom. I could no longer stand hearing her destroy Carlos. She made him sound like some sort of violent, insane murderer. It was very painful, mainly, because this description was so inaccurate of his true character and heart. The jury went behind closed doors and began their deliberations.

Carlos and I could not physically contact each other, but we were able to talk in the courtroom during the recess periods. Five hours had passed since the jury left. I was feeling sick to my stomach. I knew the Lord was with me, but I still felt so alone. I walked out into the hallway and there was a lady waiting on the outcome of her civil trial. Watching me pace back and forth, she knew from my expression, that I was under a lot of stress. The lady finally came over and started talking to me. She said, "Baby, don't be afraid. God is going to see you through." I said to her, "what if the jury finds him guilty, then what am I going to do?" I don't want them to take him away from me." She told me that I must trust in the Lord to help me to accept the outcome.

The bells had been rung. The jury had made their decision. Carlos, Mr. Peterson, Ms. Lombardo, the judge and jury all re-entered the courtroom. Judge Niemeyer asked Carlos and Mr. Peterson to stand, then she asked the jury foreman to read the verdict. And it read....WE, THE JURY, FIND CARLOS FITZPATRICK GUILTY! ON COUNT ONE, A CLASS B FELONY, DELIVERANCE OF A CONTROLLED SUBSTANCE, WE THE JURY, FIND CARLOS FITZPATRICK GUILTY! ON COUNT TWO A CLASS B FELONY, POSSESSION OF A CONTROLLED SUBSTANCE, WE THE JURY FIND CARLOS FITZPATRICK, GUILTY! ON COUNT THREE A CLASS C FELONY, RESISTING ARREST....I just stood there in a state of shock. I felt like I had just seen someone die right before my eyes. Carlos just broke down in tears and fell to his knees right in the courtroom. Some of the women on the jury panel even began to cry. The prosecuting attorney even seemed a bit weepy. I couldn't cry, I couldn't do anything. I waited for the guards to take Carlos back to the change room, so that I could get his clothes and I waited for Mr. Peterson. He was heartbroken; he didn't know what to say to me. All I could say was thank you, Mr. Peterson, you did your very best and keep us in our prayers. Mr. Peterson said he would file the necessary paperwork for us to appeal the conviction and would try his best to ask Judge Niemeyer to be merciful at the sentencing. As I walked to the car, I could feel one of those panic attacks coming on but I refused to let it happen. I began to plead the blood of Jesus. That's one thing I remembered from when I first became acquainted with the Pentecostal church. We were taught whenever you were faced with fear, just begin to say the blood of Jesus, the blood of Jesus and demons and the spirits would flee. I managed to drive myself home without freaking out, as I listened to my Christian tapes in the car. The Lord kept me safe and calm all the way home.

When I got to Momma and Daddy's house, everyone was waiting to hear the news. I had talked so much about how the Lord was going to give us a miracle and we had prayed and fasted continually before the Lord, asking for his grace and

Gwendolyn Jackson

mercy. Now I had to walk in here and tell them that Carlos was found guilty. I didn't understand why the Lord seemed to have turned his back on us, not answering one prayer regarding this trial. At one point it seemed like we had broken through when Lee Jordan testified to his guilt of selling the drugs, but even that testimony was not good enough for the jury to acquit Carlos. Lord, why? I wanted to know. Then the Lord said to me in that quiet still voice, ***"My word will not return to me empty, but will accomplish what I desire and achieve the purpose for which I sent It." Isaiah 55:11 (NIV)*** That word gave me immediate consolation. I had enough strength and courage to go in and break the news. Everyone was of course disappointed and felt not only Carlos, but for me as well. I was nine months pregnant and more than likely, my husband to be was on his way to prison.

Brian Jr. was very upset because he had a pretty good understanding as to what had taken place, even though he was only eight and a half years old. He and Carlos had a special relationship. They had become very good friends, had a lot of fun together and he realized things were no longer going to be the same. He was saying his prayers every night asking God to bring Carlos back home, but it didn't happen. I had to explain to Brian Jr., that sometimes God doesn't do what we ask him to do, right when would like him to, but God never makes mistakes and everything would be all right. Carlos called. He was absolutely hysterical. He was so upset, that he began to hyperventilate. I kept telling Carlos to calm down; that it was going to be O.K. I love you, I'm here for you, Jesus loves you, He knows what's best. Before long, Carlos began to calm down and regain his composure. Carlos kept saying, Denise I am so sorry that you have had to go through all of this and most of all, that I am not going to be with you and our newborn son. Carlos continued to weep and I wept quietly as we finished our conversation about what had just happened in our lives.

The sun was starting to set on another cool autumn evening. As I was driving home with Brian Jr. and trying to comfort him regarding what had transpired with Carlos; to answer the many questions that a young mind would have; his usual bright and happy smile slowly returned. Brian Jr. was a very special child, despite all the changes he had gone through with his mother and all her various lovers. It had been just the two of us, with the exception of the men that were in and out of our lives. Brian Jr. would always tell me how happy he was that he, Carlos and I were going to be one happy family. Now he had to go through another disappointment. I am learning that my choices and decisions, whether good or bad, affect not only me , they also affect my child as well. I was starting to learn that especially after this experience. Brian Jr. and I stopped for pizza and we called it a day.

When I fell down on my knees to pray that night, I began to ask the Lord, Why? I said, Lord, we prayed according to your word. I didn't understand what had happened today. I laid on the side of my bed praying to the Lord. I couldn't open my mouth, but I was praying within my spirit, because my heart was overwhelmed. All I could do was allow my spirit to make intercession for me. I had never felt so helpless and alone for there was nothing I could do to help Carlos. I could only continue trusting in God and asking him to give us strength to make it one day at a time.

By the grace of God, the days following Carlos' conviction were more peaceful than I had ever imagined they could be. I was able to sleep at night without waking up having panic attacks or crying fits. Carlos' homeboy, D.J. offered to come everyday and drive me to and from work until I went into labor. I really appreciated him doing that. Out of all of his so-called homeboys, D.J. was the only one that looked out for me. I told D.J. that the Lord was going to bless him and he would always say, that's for damn sure. I told him I don't use cuss words when talking about the Lord and he would say excuse me Lord. It was my first morning back to work since Carlos' trial began. God had really given me favor with my employer. I had missed a total of eight working days during the course of his trial. I went into my supervisor's office and closed the door. I began to explain to her the reason behind my recent absences. She had met Carlos on a few occasions. By the time I finished telling her the entire story, she was in a state of shock. She could not believe that I sat there day after day, working as though everything was completely normal and looking like a beautiful summer peach receiving plenty of rest and tender loving care. It was the Lord who sustained me. My supervisor proceeded to call the home office and tell them what had happened to me, which I really didn't want her to do, but she said she had to. These people must have been heaven sent. The home office gave my supervisor permission to pay me for every day that I was absent, even though I did not have any available sick leave or vacation time left. My supervisor and her superiors told me to let them know if I needed anything or if they could be of any assistance to me and my children. That really touched my heart and I told them that I would be eternally grateful for their kindness and understanding in this matter. I went back to my desk and just sat for a moment wondering, why were these people being so nice and understanding, normally in a case like ours, people tend to shy away from you, but they were reaching out to me. In that quiet, still voice, I heard the Lord saying I am with you. I just said Thank you Lord and went back to work.

The fall of the year is the best. I love the sunny, cool, crisp, morning air. I had decided to spend the night at Momma and Daddy's house. The baby was due in six days (which was, coincidentally, also Brian Sr.'s birthday-an omen?-just kidding!). When I woke up, I felt constipated. I went and knocked on Momma's door and told her that I had a lot of pressure on my back side and maybe today was the day. Momma wasn't sure what to think, since I came exactly on my due date the first time; but that really didn't mean anything, because each baby is different. I went ahead and got dressed for work and D.J. picked me up at his usual time. He had really been a blessing to the bitter end. When I got in the car, I told D.J. that I was having a few pains and he said he wasn't delivering any babies and I had

Thy Maker Is Thy Husband

better go back to the crib. I told D.J. it didn't make sense for me to stay home, I needed to work as long as I could to get my benefits. When I got to work, the pains kept coming. I didn't want to say anything, because women get so hyper when it comes to other women in labor. My plans were to work until I couldn't work any longer and I think I accomplished that.

I took my watch off my arm and started to keep a close watch on my contractions. They were coming about every five to seven minutes. The pains were more in my lower back and bottom, which was a lot different than the first time. I kept working feverishly on my computer trying to get just a few more things taken care of. Finally, I told my supervisor to come over to my desk and I told her that I thought that I was in labor. Total chaos broke loose in the office. Everyone began running over to my desk, asking me a thousand and one questions all at once. I finally had to tell everyone to calm down. I wanted to finish typing, printing and mailing one last letter. The ladies were practically pushing me out of my chair, when all at once, my friend Gina yelled, Denise do you want me to call Carlos for you? I immediately looked at my supervisor Charlene, because she was the only one that knew my present situation. I told her no, my friend Donna, who worked right down the street, would take me to the hospital once I called my doctor. Within an hour my contractions were three to four minutes apart and I knew it was time to get going. I knew that my coworkers were wondering why in the world Carlos wasn't coming to get me. It was very painful going through this without Carlos. I couldn't even talk to him on the phone to let him know what was going on. Donna was going to attempt to call the prison in Northern Missouri where Carlos had been taken to see if they would give him an urgent message, but until she called, Carlos would have no idea that I was about to deliver.

Donna and I arrived at the hospital, my sister Joyce was there. The nurse checked me out to make sure that I was in active labor and that I had began to dilate. Sure enough, it was on! Donna called up to the prison and the caseworker was kind enough to relay the message to Carlos, even though he was not able to make telephone calls. At least he would know that his baby was on the way. Within a couple of hours I had an entourage in the birthing room. It was like a party was going on. My brother Martise came. He brought his dinner and sat on the floor. There was plenty of laughter and humor going on in that room. It was amazing that, despite the traumatic events that Carlos and I had experienced, that so much joy and peace was in that room. Again, the presence of God was surely guarding my heart and comforting me with his tender loving care.

The labor pains got stronger. I still had my glasses on, because I wanted to see what Victor Newman was doing on the "Young and the Restless". Victor was my favorite character on the show. The soaps helped me take my mind off my circumstances so I watched them from time to time. Anyway, my bottom side was really hurting, BIG TIME! Right before I was about to deliver, Carlos called saying he had been brought back to St. Louis County to receive his sentence. He had called and finally reached my mom at home, where she was keeping Brian Jr. when he found out I was in labor. Carlos had gotten permission from the county jail superintendent to call the hospital. They even allowed him to go into their office to use the telephone. That was a blessing and a miracle. Again, in the midst of this situation, God made a way for Carlos to be as close as possible to us; to be in town for our baby's birth. Carlos said a prayer for me and I told him it was time for me to get down to business. I had dilated the full ten centimeters required to push the baby out. The head nurse had paged Dr. Martinez and he called back from his cellular phone. He was stuck in traffic on the freeway, so they said he asked if I could hold the baby for a few minutes. NOT! I really wanted my own doctor to deliver the baby, but I could wait no longer. The room was cleared with the exception of Donna, Joyce and the medical staff. My labor nurse and a staff doctor had to deliver. With just a couple of hard pushes, the baby was born. A beautiful baby boy. Carlos had his first son and for that matter, his first child born into this

Thy Maker Is Thy Husband

world. He wasn't able to share in this blessed event, but at least he was close by.

We had already picked out a boy's name. We named our son Carlos Terrell Fitzpatrick. I didn't care for Carlos' middle name at all, so we didn't make him a Jr. It was nice that all my family and friends came and supported me that day. Some of Carlos' relatives came as well, which was really special to me. After the baby and I were settled in our room, I thought about all that had happened. There was a sofa bed in my room for the father, but my baby's father couldn't be here on our child's first night in the world. It was a very sad moment for me. I couldn't believe all this had happened and my son's father was in prison on the day of his birth. I could only continue to believe the Lord knew what was best for us. The guard allowed Carlos to call me again. This time, when he called, I was really down. I told him that it hurt so badly, going through this without him. I felt so helpless, but there was nothing we could do about it. Carlos just reminded me that God was kind enough to allow him to be near us even though he couldn't be with us. I told him how beautiful the baby was. He had beautiful skin and lots of curly black hair. We were able to talk a few more minutes, then Carlos had to go. I laid there in bed with my baby and before long we drifted off to sleep.

The following day, Carlos' homeboy, D.J., came by to check on me and the baby. I saw something different in D.J. that day. I saw that beneath that hard core, "Boyz in the Hood" demeanor, D.J. had compassion. For so long my mind was programmed to believe that guys like him didn't care about anyone but themselves. But I was finding out that he and Carlos both only needed someone to show them that they cared and to show them true and sincere love. Love reciprocates. I told D.J. that I really appreciated all that he had done for us and someday I would do something special for him to show our gratitude for all of his help and time. He smiled and said, just look out for my dog, Little D. When I told him Carlos and I had given up our nicknames as part of our dedication to God, D.J. said it was time

Gwendolyn Jackson

for him to go; that I was getting ready to start that preaching stuff again. He left, but as he was leaving , he told me, all kidding aside, Denise, take care of yourself. The big G upstairs will make everything all right for you and my boy and someday we might be deacons together in the church. As the door closed, I said quietly to myself, yeah, someday.

It had been four days since the birth of baby Carlos. The first couple of days had been good, so far. This baby was so peaceful; he hardly cried. Carlos was still in the county jail. If it hadn't been so cold outside, I would have taken the baby to the jail to see him. Carlos' sentencing hearing was early Monday morning and I wanted to be there so badly, but I couldn't leave the house that soon. My entire family went to the hearing and my brother, Martise was going to testify on Carlos' behalf. All I could do was pray for God's mercy and grace that his sentence would not be harsh.

Time passed slowly. Every time the phone rang, my heart skipped a beat. When finally the call came, it was Martise. I could tell by his tone of voice, that the news wasn't good. "Thirty five years! I am really sorry Denise, we tried everything that we knew to do that could possibly soften the judge's heart, but she gave him no mercy. They literally threw the book at him! he cried. Mr. Peterson was devastated with the time given. Of course, Carlos was not doing well when we left. He just fell to his knees right in front of the judge's bench." I wasn't sure what I felt at that time. Martise told me to remember that delay doesn't mean denial. I thanked Martise for going on my behalf and told him to pray for my strength and for Carlos as well.

A few minutes later, Carlos called. He was still very upset and began to sob. He said he felt like the world was coming to an end for him; that he couldn't imagine being away from us for so many years. I had no answer for him. Tears just trickled down my face as I listened to the man I loved expressing so much fear, hopelessness and disappointment. I told Carlos to remember all the prayers we had prayed over the last seven months. They had not gone unanswered. Maybe things didn't

Thy Maker Is Thy Husband

go the way we thought they would and maybe we couldn't see God working on our behalf right now. The only way that we were going to make it through this ordeal was if we continued to walk close to the Lord and stand on His word. The Lord promised us that He would deliver us from our troubles *(Psalm 34:19 NIV)*. Carlos asked the guard for five more minutes and the guard was gracious enough to let him have the time on the telephone. He didn't quite know how to express himself, but he said to me, "Denise, today I have received a very long prison sentence and I cannot expect you to put your life on hold for my mistakes. I want you to know that I will understand if you decide that you cannot go through this any longer. The life of an inmate's wife is a very difficult one. If you choose not to wait, I won't be bitter. I will always know that you love me and cared enough to hang in there this long. Just please take good care of the boys for me. I am so sorry to have taken you through all of this. God finally gave me the family I dreamed of having and look what has happened. I am being taken away from them for a very long time. So, Denise, please tell me now, are you going to leave me?" I responded to Carlos' question, "Honey, for many years now, I have been running in and out of relationships, trying to find that special someone to love me and my son. I compromised God's ways when I knew without a doubt the end would be destruction. After we met, I felt I had finally found that special someone I had been searching for, only for it to end up in such devastation. I am here for the duration. The Lord has been preparing me for this the last few days and that's why I didn't take the news so hard. The Lord just kept telling me in my spirit to, *"be still and know that I am God," (Psalms 46:10)*. Carlos, I know that God did not intend for us to meet to fall into sin. However, I allowed myself to be tricked and be manipulated by Satan and allowed him to almost destroy me. But God was still with me in my disobedience. Now my time has come to be chastened by the Lord, because He chastens those that he loves. Until He says different, we are going through this together." Carlos continued weeping and we prayed a prayer for strength and courage. We said our good-byes. I hung up the phone and fell to my knees. I said, "Lord, in a strange way, I understand what's going on in me. You want me to know you in a real way. You want an up close and personal relationship with me. I have just been hit with the one two punch; and the right blow has finally knocked me back into the ring, to fight the good fight of faith; to run the race that was set before me."

CHAPTER 9

THE POTTER'S HOUSE

The word which came from Jeremiah from the Lord: ***Arise and go down to the potter's house and here I will cause you to hear my words (Jeremiah 18:2).*** Carlos and I both had arrived at the potter's house. Reality had set in. Until now, the Lord spoke to us and we could not hear him. The Lord had been patient and long suffering, but we still would not hear his voice. We left the Lord no alternative but to send us to the potter's house, where He would cause us to hear his words.

I knew without a shadow of a doubt, that I was being reshaped into another vessel, because the original plan had been spoiled. My other trips to the refiners' fire did not burn off all of the dross of my hidden sins and wounded heart. This trip to the oven was going to be hotter and much more severe than before. I knew that I had no place to run back to; that all I could do was endure what I had to. This reminded me of labor. I had to endure the pain. That was the hard cold facts!

My fiancée had just been given thirty five years; I had two children to raise alone; my finances were a total disaster—depleted by legal fees and doctor bills. The company I worked for was going through financial difficulties and their future seemed a bit bleak. Nothing was going in my favor. The odds were definitely against me. This was no time for me to run scared, since the Lord promised me that I would not run away from this test. I had heard time and time again, that the Lord is not like our educational system, He doesn't just push us on through when we don't pass the test. We must try again and again until we pass the test victoriously.

Not long ago, I remember Kayla's husband saying, "Denise, the Lord is trying to tell you to stop right now and seek His face. You will not be able to handle too much more of this emotionally. The devil is trying to destroy you and if you don't

Gwendolyn Jackson

take the time to get away by yourself and seek the Lord, the enemy is going to destroy you spiritually, emotionally and mentally." I was frightened. In other words, the Lord's patience with me had worn thin. He could have destroyed me then, but because of his unfailing love, He did not give up. He decided to take me to the potter's house. I began to see so clearly, this wasn't just about Carlos, but it was about me too.

I called the prosecuting attorney's office to see if Ms. Lombardo would meet with me concerning Carlos' sentence. To my surprise, she agreed to meet with me. I had no resentment towards her and understood perfectly well that she was just doing her job. I believe Carlos understood that as well, he just didn't understand why she wanted him to serve so much time. My Aunt Rose, Baby Carlos and I went to meet with her. Ms. Lombardo was very pleasant and I am quite sure she thought the same of me. She felt that I was a victim of circumstance. Ms. Lombardo and I met in her office to discuss any alternatives that Carlos had. At that point, Ms. Lombardo was done prosecuting the case and any type of reprieve could only come through the courts or the governor's office. After discussing a few things with her, she said the strangest thing to me. She said, "Everything will be O.K., it will all work out." I accepted that as being a word of assurance and comfort from the Lord and we concluded our meeting. Afterwards, she asked permission to hold the baby, which I allowed. I thank God, that He gives us the strength and the ability to forgive and love despite the injustices that are done to us. It was amazing that the woman who sent this child's father to prison for a very long time, held his son before he did. I told her thanks for her time and God bless and we went our way.

It was time to return to work, but I didn't want to leave the baby. This little person, I thought, had no idea of all of the turmoil and tragedy that had taken place in the lives of his parents that year. During my entire pregnancy, I prayed and asked God to keep me sane and in good health so that I could take good care of my children and He had done just that. During

Thy Maker Is Thy Husband

my time off, I only received fifty percent of my salary, but I also received many gifts and financial blessings from my parents, employer and friends. I didn't want to go to Pastor Richards' I couldn't face telling him another tragic tale. It was difficult enough going to him telling him that I had fallen and become pregnant. There was no way I was going to tell him that Carlos had now gone off to prison. So I really didn't have my church family to support me during this time, but the Lord still provided.

My first day back at work was weird. I wasn't sure who knew what had happened to me. The supervisor from the office across the street was an alternate juror at the time and maybe she was afraid enough not to blabber my business all over the office; but she was definitely the gossip columnist of the office. The Lord told me to walk into that office with my head held high; that He would never leave me or forsake me; and I did just that. I wasn't sure how much I would be able to concentrate and be productive, but all I could do was take one day at a time.

The boys and I began to adjust to our new lifestyle. It was very different having a newborn baby after almost nine years. I was depending on the Lord for everything each and every day. I needed Him to rock me to sleep at night, when I laid down and thought about Carlos being in prison. Each day when I went in to work, I managed to go in with a smile on my face, looking like a woman without any worries in the world. I began to see something in God even though I knew I was going through the refiner's fire. It astonished me that I could go into work each day; be more productive than anyone in the office; not stressed out; go home each day, be up half the night nursing baby Carlos; deal with Carlos being away; and be as strong as I was. I asked the Lord to show me in His word, then He showed me something. *"The Lord will strengthen your frame. You will be like a well watered garden; like a spring whose waters never fail."* **(Psalms 58:11).** It was Him [the Lord] doing it. The Lord showed me that as I yielded to Him that I would continue to increase my strength both naturally and spiritually.

Gwendolyn Jackson

The Christmas holiday was upon us once again. It was hard to imagine, that this time last year, Carlos, Brian Jr. and I was out Christmas shopping together and doing all of those fun things that go on during the holiday season. But time had definitely brought about a change. Carlos was in a prison cell clear across the state. We hadn't been able to talk to him on the phone in over a month and he had only been able to see his son in the pictures that I mailed to him. We knew that God was doing something in both of our lives and we had to continue on the path the Lord had laid for us. I really wanted Carlos to see his baby boy and I knew the Lord heard my heart's cry.

Out of nowhere, one day, a collect call from Carlos came from the county jail. I was so excited to hear his voice, I exclaimed, "Carlos, what are you doing here?"

He said, "Denise, they said they think they brought me down here by mistake." We both knew it wasn't a mistake; that God had made a way for him to see his son. The next visiting day, the children and I went out to the county jail and Carlos saw his son for the very first time behind the prison cell glass. It was touching and heartbreaking at the same time. I got myself together and we enjoyed our one hour visit through the glass talking on those gross telephones (I made sure I brought alcohol pads to disinfect them). The hour flew by and we had to say goodbye to Carlos. Carlos remained in the county jail four days and we were able to talk each and every day. It was four days before Christmas when they sent him back across the state. We both thanked and praised God that at least he was near us during the holidays. We counted that as a blessing.

The children and I shopped for the Christmas holiday. This year was going to be as close to normal as all the other Christmas days. I was determined not to be in a depressed mood or to allow the situation to get the best of me. Brian Jr. and I put up our Christmas tree and decorated it with festive holiday lights. We picked out pretty ornaments and carefully placed each one on our tree. We pulled the Christmas stockings out of the box and hung them over the fireplace. We put the stocking we made for Carlos last year up first and we also added a stocking for baby Carlos. We were going to have a blessed Christmas even though we didn't have a lot money and Carlos was away. We had already received our Christmas blessings.

God allowed me to go through the pregnancy without any complications whatsoever. He was supplying our basic needs each day; and I was in my right mind. Most people who had gone through what I had just experienced would have been under psychiatric counseling and taking daily doses of Prozac, Valium, or Paxil. But God promises us in His word, that He hasn't given us the spirit of fear, but of power, love and a sound mind. A SOUND MIND. The enemy would come to me from time to time and tell me that my experiences were going to make me have a nervous breakdown. I sometimes wondered if I would. Then the Lord would immediately give me something from His word to contradict the lies that Satan tried to tell me.

The family had the annual Christmas breakfast at Mom and Dad's. We had our usual homemade biscuits, stewed sweet potatoes, grits, slab bacon and all of that old southern style cooking. The question of the day of course was, how is Carlos doing? I was beginning to feel a little more comfortable talking about it. It was sort of difficult once you had established a reputation of being this stable woman of God, to end up in the big mess that I was in. But just like we got into the mess, we were sure God was going to bring us out, in His own time. The family was most gracious to the children and me and everyone seemed to have a genuine concern about Carlos, which I really appreciated. After a day of festivities, the children and I returned to our house and enjoyed the rest of the evening. I thought that I would be sad and tearful, but I wasn't – it turned out to be a very blessed day. I took the baby to see Carlos' grandmother and she and Carlos' aunt, blessed the children with fifty dollars. I knew that when I wrote Carlos and told him how his family blessed the children, that he would be very moved. Carlos always felt that his family didn't care about him or his child, but they made an effort to show love and support. That's

Gwendolyn Jackson

what Christmas is about; showing our love to each other as God showed us.

Nineteen ninety three was a hell of a year for me and I was certain that I was going to bring the New Year in on the right note. The Lord had been dealing with me on a new level. I loved my church and Pastors Debbie and Lewis Richards, but the Lord was calling me. I couldn't imagine having to leave them, but I realized that God was taking me to another level. I had been visiting Faith Temple Church (only a few minutes from my house) off and on for the past few months. The word that was imparted into my spirit while fellowshipping at that church, gave me the necessary spiritual weapons to bear my burdens. Donna had invited me to come and visit early last year and I really enjoyed the service, for it had been years since the power of God filled me the way it did right after Carlos was convicted. The Lord was leading me to that church.

Faith Temple Church had a New Year's Eve Concert each year and Donna had invited me to go. And wouldn't you know it, I caught the flu the day before. I was as sick as a dog; coughing so hard that I literally sounded like a dog; blowing my nose until it sounded like some sick animal in distress. But I was determined to go. I took some medicine and laid down to get enough strength to get up out of the bed. By the time Donna arrived, I was able to get up and go. Satan knew that the Lord had plans for me and tried to stop me, but I had to press on. The pastor was in the foyer, greeting all of the guests as they entered. I already knew several people who belong to this church. As a matter of fact, my brother, Martise went to school with Pastor Lorenzo Jamison. Pastor Jamison was a very friendly and warm individual. He immediately made you feel welcome. As I entered the foyer, I made him remember who I was, for we had met on several other occasions. I went on to tell him that I had been praying – seeking the Lord's counsel about joining Faith Temple Church. He immediately invited me to come back to his office. The Lord impressed upon me at that time to be straight forward with Pastor Jamison. I gave him the long and short of

Thy Maker Is Thy Husband

the entire scenario regarding Carlos and me. I explained to him that we would have been married by now, but the things that transpired this year didn't allow that to take place. I went on to tell Pastor Jamison that I still loved Carlos and that I believed that the Lord didn't want me to run away anymore; but to withstand this test and endure until the end.

Pastor Jamison listened intently as I went through the events that lead up to Carlos' arrest, conviction and incarceration. After taking in everything that I had said, Pastor Jamison began to speak words of encouragement to me and to share what the word of God had to say concerning our situation. I distinctly recall him telling me to read the story of Joseph in the book of Genesis. Joseph went from the pit, to the prison and finally arrived at the palace, but that was only after he had endured what he had been called upon to endure. Pastor Jamison told me to continue doing good and as I am taking care of God's business, He was going to be taking care of my mine. The pastor reminded me that individuals often get into difficult situations that only God can deliver us from. Pastor Jamison told me that as I continue to seek God with my whole heart and doing what He has commissioned me to do that I would reap in due season – if I didn't faint according to the promises given to us in the word of God. Pastor Jamison admired the fact that I was willing to go through this ordeal with Carlos; he said most women would have run away. Dealing with someone being incarcerated is not a light affliction, neither is single parenthood, but Pastor Jamison said that he believed that God would honor the fact that I was trying to do what was morally and spiritually correct; He would move on my behalf. After speaking with Pastor Jamison, my spirit was at rest that this was the Pastor that the Lord would place over my life at this time.

There was still some doubt and I didn't want to leave Pastor Lewis and Pastor Debbie. I dreaded the fact of having to build a new relationship with another Pastor. I could tell that Pastor Jamison was a lot different from Pastor Richards. Pastor Jamison was a pastor of the nineties; a mover and a shaker. He was the "get out of my way: I am coming through" type of leader, where Pastor Lewis and Pastor Debbie, were more of the parental type. I felt that the Lord did not want me clinging to any flesh; he wanted me to totally depend on Him. I knew that at any time, when my trials were getting too difficult for me to handle, that I could run to Pastor Lewis and Debbie for comfort. I wouldn't feel as comfortable with a new leader.

It was time for me to learn to lean completely on Jesus for everything. Before leaving Pastor Jamison's office, he prayed for Carlos, the children and me. He prayed that the Lord would cause all things to work together for our good and what Satan intended for evil, God would turn to good. I felt in my spirit that prayer reached the throne of God and it would not return void. God was going to do it for us in His own time.

I had to make a very important and difficult phone call. It was time for me to tell Pastor Richards that the Lord had led me to move to Faith Temple Church. There had been so much dissension in our church, that I didn't want Pastor Richards to think that was my reason for leaving. As a matter of fact, if I had my way, I would have stayed, but God was doing a new thing in my life and I had to go. I felt like a child who had finally matured. It was time for me to move to the next level and face my trials and tests head on and to discover who Jesus Christ really was to me.

When I called Pastor Richards, I didn't beat around the bush; I came right out and told him that the Lord had led me to another church. I told him the name of the church and the pastor and also explained my reason for leaving. Pastor Richards, of course, was very disappointed and saddened by the fact that I was leaving. Despite my falling from grace and becoming pregnant of out wedlock, Pastor Richards still had much faith in and respect for me. The only thing Pastor Richards said to me was that if God has told me that I must move, then I must do what God had instructed me to do. He expressed his and Pastor Debbie's sincere agape love for me and told me that I was welcome to come back at anytime, if things did not work out. I really appreciated his concern and understanding and I thanked God for giving me the wisdom to call and let them know I was leaving. These days people don't seem to have any respect for the people of God. The Christians of the nineties feel that they don't owe anyone any explanation for their actions or decisions, but that is not true. God places Pastors over us as shepherds over our souls and we must acknowledge their authority over our lives. The word of God tells us "let everything be done decently and in order".

The following Sunday, I made the transition to Faith Temple Church. I was very excited to see what God was going to do in my life. I really felt that God had promoted me to the next spiritual level. I was going to be introduced to a new spiritual curriculum with multiple tests and quizzes that I had yet to take and pass victoriously. God knew that I had to be assigned to a different shepherd to go through this wilderness experience. The Lord let me see that we must be obedient to His voice and his instructions, for He, Himself, equips us with everything we need to come through each and every trial. We must follow His instructions to the letter. Part of my passing this test was to be under the proper shepherd for this time in my life. We are one body in Christ, but we all have different functions and purposes.

No sooner had I changed my membership, all hell was breaking loose. Carlos' request for a new trial had been denied. We fasted and prayed night and day once again and it still was rejected. This thirty five year prison sentence was becoming more and more real to me each day. We were running out of options.

The winter had been one of the roughest and coldest that I could remember. It was so hard getting out there everyday before the break of day with two kids, in subzero temperatures, digging out of the snow and dropping them off at the babysitters' and driving across town to work. One morning as I was getting off the highway, saying morning prayer and quoting a scripture from *Psalms 34*, I looked up and saw this big, orange, beat up

Gwendolyn Jackson

truck coming right at me. He rammed right into the front of my car. I knew that I was O.K.; it was just another left hook from the devil. This man got out of his car, drunk as a skunk. No license, no insurance, nothing. He barely knew what his name was and, of course, when the police came, they didn't even take him to jail. It was a blessing anyway. At least I was able to pay my car insurance and have my repairs done and I was not hurt. So, the devil still didn't get the victory.

A few days later I was going to work doing my normal morning routine. Most days I would bring a bagel, grape juice and a banana from home for my breakfast. I was in my usual joyful mood, because the Lord gave me new joy and mercy each morning. When I walked into the office, I immediately saw my old supervisor, Charlene, in the office. She had moved back to our home office out of state and Maggie was the new office manager in charge. When I walked further into the office, I saw boxes everywhere and people packing up their desks and personal belongings. The office was closing. All I could do was laugh. I said Lord I am going to praise you anyway. The devil was trying to throw everything at me, including the kitchen sink. I proceeded to go and ask Charlene to give me some boxes as well; as I perceived that we all no longer had jobs. The human resource manager came to the office with her to discuss severance pay and other options with the employees. Charlene and the human resource manager asked me to hold off packing up my desk. They called me into the office and explained to me that due to reasons beyond their control, they were forced to close the office. However, they would like to offer me a transfer to the home office. I immediately told them that wouldn't be an option for me at this time due to my family situation. I began to leave the office and they said they would like to make me another offer. The two of them asked if I would work under contract with them on a month-to-month basis. They told me they would continue paying me my present salary. I would retain my full time status and keep all my benefits, work a five hour work day instead of seven and a half. As an added bonus, I

Thy Maker Is Thy Husband

would be paid an additional five hundred dollars a month as long as I worked under contract and met the minimum production requirements set forth in the contract. They advised me that only I and one other employee were being offered this option. Their decision was based on the trustworthiness, dependability, productivity and quality standards previously displayed. It was indeed an honor for me to be chosen by them. God had given me favor with them and the ability to be one of the best employees in the office. God had a ram in the bush for me, just as he had for Abram. This offer was definitely designed by God for me. Having a newborn baby was hard on me and God, who is so rich in mercy and compassion for his children, made a way for me to take care of this baby and have quality time to spend with both the children. Everyone else was leaving the office upset, angry and/or in tears; I however, had a testimony. The Lord had blessed me in the middle of this madness.

After I got home, I sat down and I pondered the fact that I was the only one in the department left with a job. It was amazing after all that had transpired in the past few months, that I ended up being one of the best employees in the office. My house was the only house left standing today at our office. To God be the glory.

Our journey through the potter's house continued. Carlos and I had been communicating by letter for the past five months. It was starting to hurt us both that he hadn't been able to hold his new baby boy yet. However, both Carlos and I were continuing to build our relationship with the Lord on a daily basis. It seemed like every message I heard preached, every Christian article or newsletter I read dealt with a "going through the wilderness experience", or something about the "fiery trial that you are now experiencing". I knew that God had taken me to another level with Him that I hadn't experienced before. My Aunt Rose told me that she had had dream we were on a cruise ship. The ship had taken out to sea and once we were in the middle of the ocean, I decided that I didn't want to go that way; I wanted to go back to the shore. My Aunt Rose told me that in the dream she said to me, "No Denise, you can't go back now, it's too late, you might as well go ahead and ride it on out." That was confirmation for me. I was going to be made this time in the refiner's fire and I was going to ride the tide; go through the storm; and come out on the other side. I was too far out in the spiritual sea to turn back now. Day after day, week after week and now month after month, I felt the pain and the suffering of this trial. But, I knew the Lord was with me. Carlos told me that he had been crying out to the Lord about him being closer to his family. We were told by the officials at the prison that transfers were difficult to obtain and he probably would have to remain where he was-three hundred miles from home. Carlos and I wouldn't receive that. We began to pray and to believe that God was going to make a way for him to be closer to home so the he could see his son grow up.

Within a matter of days, Carlos heard keys rattling as the guard yelled, "Fitzpatrick, transfer to Southeastern." Carlos and I had received an answer to our prayers. Carlos was being moved less than a forty minute ride from home; actually back to the same county. It was a miracle. Most inmates have to have extremely extenuating circumstances to be considered for transfer, but God moved on our behalf once again. All we did was ask and God delivered!

For several months, Carlos and I had been praying and seeking the Lord concerning our future together. When Carlos originally received the thirty year prison term, he told me that he would understand if I didn't want to go through this with him any longer. I knew that I loved Carlos, despite all the adversity we had faced in the short period of time we had been acquainted. Without a shadow of doubt, Carlos' love for me was beyond any expectations I would have had for a man. I also realized that since Carlos had been born again; that this was his first time truly experiencing and seeing true love exemplified.

Pastor Jamison and I had our first counseling sessions regarding the possibility of me marrying Carlos in prison. I knew that this would be the craziest thing in the world to do, in

Thy Maker Is Thy Husband

the natural, but when I looked into the spiritual realm, I saw God doing something else. I saw this as an opportunity to see God move in a supernatural and miraculous way. This time, I knew my flesh had nothing to gain; that this was a spiritual thing. In my human mind, I couldn't really explain why I felt compelled to marry Carlos under these circumstances, but for some strange reason, I had the peace of God that surpassed all understanding. Pastor Jamison and I had a very productive counseling session. He was very honest, telling me these were not the ideal circumstances under which we should marry. However, he appreciated the fact that we were willing to act on faith. He said our marriage would bring some stability into the lives of the children and to the both of us. Pastor Jamison gave his blessings and we planned our wedding day for June 15, the day we met two years earlier.

Meanwhile, the prison chaplain, Rev. Estes, wanted to have his counseling session with Carlos and me together. I found this to be pretty interesting, that the prison chaplain would even take enough interest in an inmate to provide premarital counseling. This guy was different. He seemed to be a pleasant man, but a bit hurried. As we waited for Carlos to come to the visiting room, he told me that he normally didn't recommend inmates to be married, but he felt different about this one. He told me that he had peace in his spirit about this one and he had to flow with the spirit. When Carlos made his arrival into the meeting room, he actually gave us a minute to greet one another with a hug and very short kiss! It was time to get down to business.

Rev. Estes had the three of us join hands for a word of prayer, then he began to explain to us the pros and cons of getting married while Carlos was still in prison. When the Bible speaks of the husband being the head of the wife and the household, it means that he is the priest of his home; the provider. He asked both of us if we understood that Carlos would not be able to fulfill that part of his obligation to his family at this time. We both agreed that we understood. Rev. Estes went on to talk about how our obligation to fulfill each other emotionally would be limited and the sexual part of our marriage would be non-existent under these conditions. When he gave us a chance to speak, I told him that I knew that those were carnal matters, but it was a spiritual matter that we were dealing with. I knew that I was not going to have all of the advantages that most married women had. I knew that all the of the burdens for the family were going to be on me and I realized that it wasn't going to be easy; but I was willing to see what the Lord was going to do in our lives through this situation. We had come too far to back out now. Carlos told Rev. Estes, that he had never felt this free in his life. Even though he was incarcerated physically, he was freer than most people on the outside of that gate. Carlos went on to say that he realized that Satan had deceived us both when we originally began our relationship. God had allowed us to meet so that he could be led to Jesus Christ; but we allowed Satan to cause us to get off track and fall short of the glory of God. Thanks be to God, who always causes us to triumph; who still gives us the victory. "Today, I am saved," Carlos continued. "A spirit-filled believer of Jesus Christ and all because this woman, sitting here, took the time to tell me who Jesus was to me and how much he could change my life. Yes, I may have gotten into trouble and ended up in here for the time being, but we are believing and standing on God's word to bring deliverance to us. Meanwhile this woman and I will join as one in Holy Matrimony."

Rev. Estes just sat there with his mouth open. He said to us, "What more can I say? Let's go for it!" He prayed for us once again, especially for my strength to continue to endure this hardship and for Carlos to be covered by the blood of Jesus as he continued to do battle in the spirit realm behind prison walls.

Carlos officially proposed to me during our next visit. We got on the platform where they take pictures and had our picture taken as he got down on one knee and proposed to me. He said, "My beautiful queen, I, first of all, want to apologize for being so stupid and not seeing this precious jewel that God had blessed me with the day that I met you. I now realize that the devil had

Thy Maker Is Thy Husband

me blinded, but thank God that today I see. I am so sorry for not being out there to take care of you and the children the way that a real man should. I promise to you today, God is my witness, that I am going to make up to you all of the heartache and pain that this has brought upon you. You didn't deserve this, but I thank God that he knew that his daughter had what it took to make it through something like this and leads someone like me to Christ. I know, because I found you as my wife, that God is going to deliver us from this situation. So, because I found you, my queen, I am going to receive favor from the Lord." After saying all that, Carlos asked me to be his wife and I accepted his proposal with honor.

Our wedding day arrived quickly. I went out and purchased two identical gold wedding bands. Donna was my matron of honor and Brian Jr. was the ring barrier. Pastor Jamison and several of the family members came to witness this event. We both told them that we realized that this was a bit unusual, but we believed God was doing something that neither one of us could explain. I wasn't dressed in the normal bridal attire. I wore my pink suit and pearl earrings and necklace. Carlos had to wear the gray pants that all inmates must wear, but he wore a light pink and gray shirt to complement my suit. Carlos couldn't believe that he was getting married. His stepmother, Mrs. Iverson, who also attended our wedding, said that she could remember the day he said wasn't ever getting married; that he was going to be a Player all his life. Pastor Jamison had the two of us join hands, as we began to repeat the vows one to the other. When Pastor Jamison repeated the part that says, "for better or worse", I thought, for a quick second, how much worse could it be? I laughed to myself. Pastor Jamison completed the vows, anointed us and began to pray fervently for us. I thanked and praised God for this, because I knew without a doubt, that we had done everything decently and in order. We had sought the counsel of the men of God. We had assurance that God was with us once again. Pastor Jamison got this funny grin on his face and told Carlos to salute his bride. Carlos was a little shy at the moment and gave me a quick salute. Everyone began to clap, even some of the prison guards came in to witness our blessed occasion.

Of course, we didn't have the normal wedding reception and honeymoon events that usually take place. Our wedding reception menu consisted of chicken wings and french fries from the prison's vending machines and chocolate cupcakes with lemon lime soda to toast with. Carlos and I spent a few hours together after our wedding with approximately one hundred other folks in the visiting room. Then we said our good byes and Donna took the blushing bride to her bridal suite alone. I was happy on one hand, but on the other hand it was sort of frightening. Then I had to remind myself to cast down those imaginations. My name was no longer Denise Baker Turner. I became Mrs. Denise Fitzpatrick. We received a few wedding cards and words of congratulations, but I knew for the most part, that the majority of our well wishers, whom we hadn't heard from, thought I had probably gone stone zip crazy. Things of the spirit are foolishness to the carnal mind.

My life in the potter's house continued after the marriage. It had almost become comical how the devil was coming at me with one trial after another. I knew that I was being tested under severe heat and pressure. Sometimes I used to think, Lord, when will this let up? When I make it to the crazy house?" The bills were out of control. The lights got cut off, for the first time. The kids both got chicken pox at the same time. I was almost two months behind on my rent. The lawyers were calling, wanting money; my phone bill was sky high from the toll calls from Carlos; my job was on a month-to-month basis; and I had a cold for approximately six months. I was still trying to cater to help ends meet, but it just wasn't enough. I told the Lord, all this is enough to make anyone go crazy, but Lord I am trusting you. In the midst of all this, I still made every effort to remain a faithful tither. I believe everything in me was being tested. I didn't realize that our trip to the potter's house was going to be so painful. As I was suffering out here, Carlos was catching all

Thy Maker Is Thy Husband

sorts of hell on the inside. He was doing everything he could do to be a model inmate and from what I had been told, that was a very difficult thing to do. He was dodging fiery darts all the day long. He was dealing with the loneliness and isolation of being incarcerated. There were many issues from his past haunting him and God was starting to bring them to the surface. He felt very rejected and abandoned by his family. I also had a lot of unresolved issues from my past marriage and relationships. The Lord was getting to the heart of matters.

Time was moving on. The weeks were turning into months and the months into years. When this ordeal began, I didn't think I could make it one year. The next thing I knew, four years had gone by. God had done something with the both of us that was truly amazing. Our marriage had outlasted the marriage of many people we knew-even in the church. We couldn't boast for it had been more than a notion. If it hadn't been for the grace and mercy of God, we would have fallen. We had countless numbers of disappointments regarding our legal battles; my job situation finally stabilized after going through the closing and reopening, buying out, then merger of the same company. Finally the Lord blessed me with a job at a multi-billion dollar organization, with very little stress and excellent fringe benefits. Since our trip to the potter's house, the Lord had called me to the ministry. I finally heard what the Lord was saying. As far as Carlos' legal battle was concerned, I turned that entire matter over to the Lord.

One summer night, some sisters in the Lord and I were having a party line prayer meeting on the phone. The power of God was so intense that night, that when we were finished, I couldn't fall asleep. So, I grabbed my bible to calm myself (the enemy would sometimes try to attack me at night-especially with the spirit of fear). The Lord was getting ready to show me something. The Lord told me to stop at *Deuteronomy 32:36*. It blew me clean away. The Lord was telling us to take our hands off. He was letting me know that He is more than able to do whatever I need Him to do. He could only do it when He saw that I no longer trusting in my own power or efforts. The Lord had spoken.

From that point on, we had to go to another level of faith. God didn't want us depending on lawyers, politicians, or anything else but Him. He reminded us that He didn't tell us to go out, get all of these lawyers and get into all of this debt. When the Lord guides, He also provides. First of all, we both needed to repent for getting in God's way. Carlos was a bit resistant to this, because he was so sure God told him to tell me to get another lawyer. I asked him why would the Lord tell me to do something that I couldn't afford to do or didn't have the resources to get it done? So, I conducted fund raisers and such to try and raise money. It helped some, but it wasn't enough to cover all the expenses. I knew Carlos was getting desperate. He would just be sick at times, because he was missing so much of children's lives. He had a son that he hadn't spent one day at home with; whose birthdays, holidays and fun times had been missed. This was part of being at the potter's house. We had to be the odd balls at family events and other occasions where families and married couples attended functions together. We were always alone. So the pain of this was felt from both ends. Our misery was becoming our ministry. In the midst of all this, God was starting to use us in a mighty way. In prison, Carlos was leading many men to Jesus Christ. Lives of the prison inmates were being touched by the power of God. What he was doing in there began to affect the lives of many inmates' families on the outside. We were becoming a resource center; a center of hope for this forgotten group of people. In less than a year's time, I was appointed to a leadership position in our church. That was the last thing I wanted to do, but I was happy just to be in the house of the Lord and have enough sanity left to give God praise. I didn't know why the Lord allowed me to be over anything in the midst of such a hard time of testing, but Pastor Jamison assured me once again, as I began to take care of God's business, that He was going to take care of mine. From that point on, God began to stir up the gift of God that was within me. I finally accepted my long time calling to the ministry as a teacher and prophet. *"Behold, I have refined you, but not as silver; I have tried and chosen you in out of the furnace of affliction" (Isaiah 48:10).*

CHAPTER 10

THY MAKER IS THY HUSBAND

During Carlos and I four year separation of being married under our unusual circumstances, I found out that he had not been completely honest with me regarding the events that lead up to his arrest and later his conviction. All along I would tell him that God is a God of judgment and a God of justice, but we must openly confess our sins before Him and he is faithful and just to forgive us from all unrighteousness. I wanted Carlos to understand that we cannot fool God, He was there when it all happened so he knows the truth and we can't expect him to deliver you from the situation if you don't fess up to it. Carlos was not getting it. On one occasion when I went to visit him, I asked him to tell me exactly what happened on the night of his arrest. He told me the same thing he had been saying all along, but this time I wasn't buying into it. I reminded Carlos that next morning following his arrest, he told me exactly what happened and that story was the truth. Now for the past four years he has convinced himself that something totally different had taken place. I really began to feel sorry for him, being so desperate for his freedom, that he petitioned God for something that was all based on lies.

Before long, so many things began to come to light. Carlos would go into a panic if he called and I was fifteen minutes off from my arrival time home from work. He didn't want me to do anything but go to church, go to work, to the grocery store and visit him at the prison. I was starting to feel like an inmate myself. I knew that God was remaking and reshaping me, but this was not from God. It was manipulation and control, what I considered to be spiritual witchcraft. He would use the word of God to justify the things he wanted me to do. He felt that calling home and making two and three hundred dollar phone bills were ok even though he knew that I was already in financial straits.

Thy Maker Is Thy Husband

He would always refer to himself being the priest of his home and the man of the house, but he hadn't provided a loaf of bread or a gallon of milk since the day we were married. Every woman that I met at the prison was going through one dilemma or another with their husbands or boyfriends.

One day while sitting at my desk at work, the Lord spoke to me and I know this was the Lord. He said to me "This was all one big lie, but I allowed you to go through this for my own purpose and plan for your life, but now the truth is going to be revealed to you." The Lord had me confront Carlos just like that, I told him the Lord told me that he had been lying to me and I demanded truth. Carlos began to recount the events of his arrest once again and as he told me in the beginning and again that day, he was guilty as sin, but to my disbelief, a week after our conversation, he denied ever confessing his guilt to me. He acted like I was the police. From that day forward I turned on my spiritual radars and watched Carlos very carefully.

Prison environment is like none other, there is more manipulation and scheming in there than on the streets. I believe that there are brothers in there really seeking after God with their whole hearts, but yet they too need deliverance from their past and sound spiritual support and teaching.

Well the saga continued and Carlos became more transparent to me. Again I had been taken for a ride, but in different way. I was his scapegoat and he was very co-dependent upon me for his survival in prison. The last scheme he came up with was the straw that broke the camel's back. Once again we were having it out about the outrageous phone bills I was allowing him to create, I told him it had to stop or he would force me to block any of his calls from coming through. Again he used my faith and devotion to God to try to play mind games and try to manipulate me into allowing him to have his way. He wanted new clothes for the winter. I didn't understand him; everything was always about him, poor pitiful Carlos, what about the kids, what about ME!! I wouldn't give into him this time and I told him that I could not afford to send him money, pay phone bills, come and visit him and still take care of the kids and me. He was very unreasonable and very unrealistic.

Mr. Carlos took it upon him self to prey upon my family, friends and church family. A year or so ago Pastor Jamison had a meeting with the congregation and explained our situation to them. We were petitioning the Governor for Carlos' prison sentence to be reduced, several hundred church members and friends signed the petition giving their support for our cause. Carlos took it upon himself to send a secret letter to all of the individuals on the petition asking them to send money for me to him at the prison and in turn he told them he was going to send it to me. I was outraged, mainly because a week or so prior to this taking place, he told me that God was going to bless him to purchase several brand new clothing items. I responded by saying he must be expecting a big blessing, yes he was, at the hand of taking advantage of friends and family members.

Once again, I knew I had missed God, I had no business marrying Carlos in prison. As matter of fact the marriage was never real. We never spent one day together as husband and wife. I consulted several of my so called spiritual mentors before I did this and there are a lot of well meaning saints, but sometimes the counsel that they give can be detrimental to one's life.

I continued to go through with Carlos, but I began to use a little more wisdom. I wanted to see what his true motives were in all of this. I began to slow up writing the letters, I slowed down sending money, and the visits became a little further apart. He snapped. He had the nerve to give me an ultimatum, he told me that I was not a Godly women because I was not taking care of him, he wanted to control me completely. He didn't care about being married, he wanted someone to support him during his incarceration, but it was not going to be me.

It was January of 1998, I was growing day by day spiritually and the Lord was doing great things in my life. Taking me to spiritual high places. It was year number FIVE of being celibate. It was something to celebrate and praise God for. But I thought

Thy Maker Is Thy Husband

to myself, married and celibate isn't that something. I realize that's what happens when you get tired of waiting on God and just decide to go ahead and bless yourself. I know God probably sits on His throne and laughs at us because He knows when we finish we still have to wait on Him. He has to have a sense of humor to deal with us!!

In my heart of hearts I knew something was about to happen between Carlos and I. As a matter of fact, four months ago, I took his name off all of my insurance policies as the beneficiary. I didn't know why I felt the urgency to do it, but I did.

I began to really observe his behavior patterns over the next few months. Every now and then he would have fits and go off for no reason saying no one loves him or was never there for him. He was trying to make me the mother he never had in his life. I could never fill that void. He really needed the Lord to heal his emotions.

All over the country, they have workshops and conferences for women for emotional healing, but I am beginning to see that our men need just as much healing as women do from their past if not more. That's why we are seeing so much abuse in marriages and other relationships, because there has been no true deliverance. Even in our churches today, the brothers are abusing their wives as never before. They perpetrate around the church and act as though they are holy men of God, under the banner of Bishop so and so or Elder so and so or Reverend so and so, while at home they are physically, verbally and emotionally abusing their wives and children. The church has become no more than a spiritual hospital full of sick people who need healing from God. We have heard enough health, wealth and prosperity teaching for now, unless we as people of God begin to cry loud and spare not. The world will have no hope.

I asked the Lord what is going on with the church, with the families, the marriages, everything seems to be going to hell in a hand-basket, the Lord directed me to this passage of scripture. ***"Gird yourselves and lament, you priests; wail, you who minister before the altar; come, lie all night in sackcloth, you*** *who minister to my God, for the grain offering and the drink offering are withheld from the house of your God. Consecrate a fast, call a sacred assembly" (Joel 1:13-14NKJV).*

That is the problem, we have lost our first love, we bring our money and go through the motions week after week, but there has not been any true deliverance and we no longer are seeking after God with our whole hearts. And that has been the deception.

After Carlos realized that I knew where he was coming from, he didn't really try to be super spiritual with me any longer. He had the nerve to tell me if I refused to come up and bring him food on a special food visit day, that he had another woman that was willing to do so. That was all I needed to hear. After five years of being in the desert, I began to see the land flowing with milk and honey. I told him I was done, God was getting ready to bring me out. After five years of going through all of this drama with him, to the point of me almost losing everything I had, I see now that I was just a convenience and an outside connection for him. God allowed me to go through this for my making. I saw a side of life that I never had experienced before and now I have compassion for a new group of people, prison inmates and their wives, but I will never be used by Carlos Fitzpatrick another day.

I asked the Lord was this some kind of sick joke you played on me or what? He responded by saying this *"For it was good for me that I have been afflicted that I might learn of your decrees" (Psalms 119:71).*

From that point I knew I had past the test. Carlos had no use for me after I refused to continue catering to him in prison. He had threatened to divorce me in the past from behind prison bars and that was the last time he would have a chance to do that to me.

This all was such a powerful learning experience. It was life changing, it was the hardest thing that I had ever gone through, and this even beat out my ordeal with Brian Sr. This had them all beat.

Within a few months, I was back where I first began. Denise Baker. But I was a new and improved Denise Baker. Sixteen years later I had experienced so many things that could have taken me off the face of this earth, but God called me even before the foundations of the world were created. He knew at this junction in time that I would be born and I had a mission to fulfill on this earth and the demons in hell were not glad about it. Demons and demonic forces are real. For those of us like myself who tasted of the things of God and choose to go back into the world, the Bible has this to say: *"When an unclean spirit goes out of a man, he goes through dry places, seeking rest; and finding none, he says, I will return to my house from which I came and when he comes, he finds it swept and put in order, then he goes and take with him seven other spirits more wicked than himself and they enter and dwell there and that last state of that man is worse than the first." (Luke 11:24-26. NKJV).*

I understand now why I could never be delivered from the spirit of fornication. For the Bible speaks of a man and woman becoming one flesh, that happens during sexual intercourse. So if this is taking place outside of marriage, we then create soul ties with each individual that we had intercourse with thus allowing ourselves to be filled with all sorts of spirits and demonic forces for which we may not be familiar with. That leads to multiple strong-holds being on our lives. Until we seek God for true deliverance from every soul-tie and unclean spirit that we have allowed to enter in, true deliverance can never take place.

Finally, I am at rest. I told the Lord if he and I are together by ourselves for the next 20 years, that will be just great with me. The older saints never really taught the younger saints how to deal with the normal desires that God has given us, but is only lawful in a marriage relationship. They just told you to fast and pray. That the Lord would keep you if you wanted to be kept. They really never talked about it and many individuals have gone through what I've gone through and even worse. We must teach single people who desire to remain celibate, to channel those same emotions and feeling into a relationship with God and he will fulfill your desires and make you complete and whole. A vessel worthy of honor. *"Delight thyself also in the Lord and He shall give thee the desires of thine heart." (Psalms 37:4).*

NO COMPROMISE

What does it mean to be fully dependent on thee?
Does it mean hearing God's voice, but still doing your own thing?
Or feel God tugging at your heart, but you feel you're not ready to play the part?
Where does your strength in God really lie?
Certainly not in your Compromise.
Because through God's eyes, it is in Him that you should rise.
Rise to the standards where you are fully dependent on thee and not entangled in the web of deceit.
Because it is the devil you must defeat.
He's told you lies and you feel it's okay to Compromise.
Compromise your morals, your thoughts, your integrity, and your commitment to God.
But God is calling for all of you and not just the part you want to do.
Because in God's eyes, there is no Compromise.

Teisha Sims

Gwendolyn Jackson

Printed in the United States
1643